Human Nature, Interest, and Power

Human Nature, Interest, and Power

A Critique of Reinhold Niebuhr's Social Thought

TEX SAMPLE

CASCADE *Books* · Eugene, Oregon

HUMAN NATURE, INTEREST, AND POWER
A Critique of Reinhold Niebuhr's Social Thought

Copyright © 2013 Tex Sample. All rights reserved. Except for brief quotations in critical publications or reviews, no part of this book may be reproduced in any manner without prior written permission from the publisher. Write: Permissions, Wipf and Stock Publishers, 199 W. 8th Ave., Suite 3, Eugene, OR 97401.

Cascade Books
An Imprint of Wipf and Stock Publishers
199 W. 8th Ave., Suite 3
Eugene, OR 97401

www.wipfandstock.com

ISBN 13: 978-1-62032-626-8

Cataloguing-in-Publication data:

Sample, Tex.

    Human nature, interest, and power : a critique of Reinhold Niebuhr's social thought / Tex Sample.

        xvi + 170 pp. ; 23 cm. Includes bibliographical references and index.

        ISBN 13: 978-1-62032-626-8

        1. Niebuhr, Reinhold, 1892–1971. 2. Christian realism and political problems. 3. Power (Christian theology). I. Title.

BX4827.N5 S2 2013

Manufactured in the U.S.A.

To the Valley Interfaith Project,
Phoenix, Arizona

Contents

Preface: For the Love of Niebuhr   ix

Acknowledgments   xiii

Abbreviations   xv

1 Human Nature: The Transcendent and Finite Self   1
2 Niebuhr's View of Interest   34
3 Niebuhr's Concept of Power   68
4 The Balance of Power in Niebuhr's Social Thought   85
5 Internal Power: A Brief Excursus on Formation in Niebuhr   111
6 A Narrative Illustration   119
7 Political Implications   136

Bibliography   163

Index   167

Preface

For the Love of Niebuhr

IN THE EARLY 1960S as a student at The Boston University School of Theology I crossed the Charles River and went upstream to take a course on Christian ethics at The Harvard Divinity School with Reinhold Niebuhr. By then he was, of course, a significant national figure, having been an important political realist on the national scene and active with Americans for Democratic Action. He had appeared on the cover of *Time* magazine and was a frequent contributor to both religious and secular journals and magazines. Prominent in the work of the World Council of Churches and other ecumenical efforts, he was a widely sought after speaker on college campuses, in church events and other venues. He had taught at Union Theological Seminary from the time he left his pastorate in Detroit in 1928 up until his retirement from there in 1960. He had written, as we used to say, "a shelf full of books." To a young graduate student like me he was "famous." But, I still was not prepared for the oratorical power, the charisma, and the persuasive ways in which he would captivate us.

Still affected by a series of strokes that had begun in 1952, one arm hung down at his side as he paced back and forth before the class, bursting the air with that powerful voice, hacking away and theatrically flailing the air with the other hand and arm—and, to add even further gravity to his remarks, he would sometimes growl them out in a voice that seemed in part composed of gravel. I shall never forget the day he was lecturing on human nature and shouted out, in a voice that sounded like a rock-covered beach washing away in a flood, "All of human existence is the clawing up of a huge mountain of human flesh from which you can spit down on everybody else's head!"

For the Love of Niebuhr

I began by trying to take down everything he said, but soon I was so caught up in the rhetorical force of his lecture that I simply gave up trying to write—which had a negative impact on my grade—and from that point on I simply wrote down "quotable quotes," so that my notebook looked like the work of an ethnographer collecting proverbs, aphorisms, and a host of other sayings from some kind of poignant cultural event of an unusually dramatic kind. I was captured.

From that point on, I would be a "Niebuhrian." For the next thirty years he informed my efforts in the civil rights movement, shaped my response to the issues of peace and justice, characterized the way in which I participated in community agencies and events, and, of course, framed the courses that I taught in theological ethics, church and society, and strategies of social change.

Later I read Ludwig Wittgenstein for the first time. It embarrasses me to say so, but I came to him very late. My philosopher had been Alfred North Whitehead and my theology was a process one. My engagement with Wittgenstein led me to Alasdair MacIntyre, to a reworking of John Howard Yoder, to Stanley Hauerwas, and, of course, to many others. Sometime during all of that I read Michel Foucault and more recently I worked intensively with anthropologists Talal Asad and Saba Mahmood. All of these shaped the ways in which I began to rethink a range of questions and issues.

Yet, my work has not been only scholarly. For the past ten years I have been heavily invested in broad-based organizing in Phoenix, Arizona. My intellectual study and my engagement in organizing led me not only to question Niebuhr, but to move into a more detailed and close examination of the issues of the human condition, justice, power, interest, and the role of the church. I found Niebuhr's view of human nature increasingly unhelpful. It simply did not fit so many of the people and circumstances in which I found myself. To add to the problem, the entire notion of interest or self-interest grew increasingly complicated, and I found the concept of interest in Niebuhr's terms not adequate to the range of concerns I encountered, for example, in broad-based organizing. To make matters worse, Niebuhr's notion of the balance of power—even his concept of power—simply did not match up with a more relational understanding of power and the more material, down-on-the-ground dynamics of power I engaged. To be sure, non-reciprocal patterns of power are quite clear, but even the notion of balance itself became abstract, seemingly a concept from another time and place. Previously in my life I had found Niebuhr to be the most "empirical"

For the Love of Niebuhr

theologian I had ever read. But increasingly his once compelling generalizations about the self, its pursuit of self-interest, its will to power, and the necessary search for a balance or equilibrium of power seemed to be high on a ladder of abstraction and not engaged with concrete forms of life. Strangely, he was ahistorical.

Somewhere in all of that I ceased being a Niebuhrian. It was a difficult divorce. I still love the man, at least the kind of power, charisma, and compelling stature that I engaged in that spring of so many years ago. I feel a strange infidelity in criticizing him. To be perhaps too candid, I feel in this essay that I will be criticizing "an old friend"—and really, beyond that, a master of the trade who taught me skills that shaped the very way that I worked in the world. In fact, it feels like a betrayal. I hope I will be able to portray this sense of my indebtedness to Niebuhr as I work along in this manuscript. Let me say, too, that I hope not to come off like some smart-ass who thinks he's more intelligent than Niebuhr, or more sophisticated. I hope that I have benefited from thought that was not available to Niebuhr, and that my concerns are to address issues he raised in ways that reflect some very helpful ideas that came along later.

Then why focus on Niebuhr? Why not just lay out a point of view and leave the great man alone? The basic reason is that I find his thought so powerfully present among so many community activists and, for that matter, academics. It is because of this that I engage Niebuhr in this book.

Finally, the Niebuhr corpus is vast. I cannot hope in this space to do a thoroughgoing treatment of his thought. Rather, this is an essay on his social thought. While other aspects of his work will inevitably enter into these discussions, I will not address his theology or his ethics as such. Fine treatments of these already exist. My focus will be on three of his basic concepts: human nature, interest, and power.[1] With respect to these three concepts, I contend that none of them can any longer be used in the way that Niebuhr used them. They require reconfiguration or perhaps abandonment entirely. In the first chapter I will turn to his view of human nature.

---

1. For a good summary of criticisms of Niebuhr, see Rasmussen, *Reinhold Niebuhr*, 16–41. I will not address these criticisms here because I will be coming from a different direction in addressing Niebuhr's social thought. I do find especially telling the critique by Beverly Harrison, *Making the Connections*, 54–80. Her conclusions about Niebuhr's misreading of Marx are quite compelling, in my view.

Acknowledgments

THE CONTENTS OF CHAPTERS 1 through 4 were presented in an earlier form as The Schooler Lectures at The Methodist Theological School in Ohio in September 2011. I am grateful to President Jay Rundell and Academic Dean Randy Litchfield for their kind invitation to be the Schooler Lecturer and for their warm hospitality.

I regard critique as a gift. None of us ever gets things right, so far as I can tell, and only through the criticism of others do we gain the capacity to move in a more intelligible direction. To the extent that what I write here is intelligible, it is due to very constructive criticism I have received from a number of people.

Stanley Hauerwas has always been more generous in his response to my work than it merits, but I deeply appreciate his comments on the manuscript and his suggestions for improvement. Larry Rasmussen, a sagacious interpreter of Niebuhr, offered very helpful criticisms and proposed that I write a last chapter on the political implications of this study, which I did. I think he was exactly right about the necessity of such a chapter, and I am grateful for his contribution. Ernesto Cortés, Jr., also made important suggestions that improved the manuscript, but my indebtedness to him as mentor in broad-based organizing goes well beyond his attention to this text.

I am especially indebted to Yvonne Zimmerman. Not only did she do a line-by-line editing of the manuscript, she raised many questions requiring greater clarification. She offered any number of suggestions on places to cut the manuscript where I had gone into far too much detail. Even further, my syntax, always in need of help, greatly benefited from her suggestions for rephrasing, for more explicit statement, and for a more felicitous style. Because of her work, the prose in this book is better than I can write.

This is my second time to work with Jacob Martin as copy editor. It is a gift to have him read my manuscripts. His careful eye for detail, for nuances of meaning, for finding the right word, for clearing up my confusions, for

Acknowledgments

pursuing footnote references for accuracy, and for attention to the myriad things a copy editor does are greatly appreciated.

With gifts of criticism as fine as all of these, I alone remain responsible for what is finally in this text. I have always had better friends than I deserve, and this is certainly true here.

I am also indebted to the Valley Interfaith Project, an Industrial Areas Foundation broad-based organizing effort in greater Phoenix, where I have been engaged for the past decade. It is in this setting that I have learned much about human subjects, interest, and power. I have been tutored by Joe Rubio, lead organizer of VIP, and by a number of other organizers and staff with whom I have worked: Connie Andersen, Katherine Hoff, Timothy McManus, Jorge Montiel, Paula Osterday, and Laura Rambicur. Because of my deep indebtedness to VIP, its organizers and leaders, I dedicate this book to them.

As in anything I do, Peggy Sample is utterly indispensable. She deals with a wide range of life and love with laughter, energy, and unfailing faithfulness. That I get to live with her is more than I could ever have dreamed.

Abbreviations

BP	*The Balance of Power: History and Theory*. Michael Sheehan. London: Routledge, 1996.
CCAS	*Capitalism and Christianity, American Style*. William E. Connolly. Durham: Duke University Press, 2008.
CLCD	*The Children of Light and the Children of Darkness: A Vindication of Democracy and a Critique of Its Traditional Defense*. Reinhold Niebuhr. New York: Scribner's, 1944.
CPP	*Christianity and Power Politics*. Reinhold Niebuhr. New York: Scribner's, 1940.
CRNR	*Christian Realism and the New Realities*. Robin Lovin. Cambridge: Cambridge University Press, 2008.
DP	*Discipline and Punishment: The Birth of the Prison*. Michel Foucault. New York: Vintage, 1977.
EAC	*Essays in Applied Christianity*. Reinhold Niebuhr. Selected and edited by D. B. Robertson. New York: Living Age, 1959.
ERN	*The Essential Reinhold Niebuhr: Selected Essays and Addresses*. Reinhold Niebuhr. Edited by Robert McAfee Brown. New Haven: Yale University Press, 1986.
FH	*Faith and History: A Comparison of Christian and Modern Views of History*. Reinhold Niebuhr. New York: Scribner's, 1949.
FS	*Formations of the Secular: Christianity, Islam, Modernity*. Talal Asad. Stanford: Stanford University Press, 2003.
FR	*The Foucault Reader*. Michel Foucault. Edited by Paul Rabinow. New York: Pantheon, 1984.
GR	*Genealogies of Religion: Discipline and Reasons of Power in Christianity and Islam*. Talal Asad. Baltimore: Johns Hopkins University Press, 1993.
MMIS	*Moral Man and Immoral Society: A Study in Ethics and Politics*. Reinhold Niebuhr. New York: Scribner's, 1932.

Abbreviations

MNHC	*Man's Nature and His Communities: Essays on the Dynamics and Enigmas of Man's Personal and Social Existence.* Reinhold Niebuhr. New York: Scribner's, 1965.
NDM	*The Nature and Destiny of Man.* 2 vols. Reinhold Niebuhr. New York: Scribner's, 1941–43.
ON	*On Niebuhr: A Theological Study.* Langdon Gilkey. Chicago: University of Chicago Press, 2001.
PI	*The Passions and the Interests: Political Arguments for Capitalism before Its Triumph.* Albert O. Hirschman. Princeton: Princeton University Press, 1977.
P/K	*Power/Knowledge: Selected Interviews and Other Writings, 1972–1977.* Michel Foucault. Edited by Colin Gordon. New York: Pantheon, 1977.
PP	*Politics of Piety: The Islamic Revival and the Feminist Subject.* Saba Mahmood. Princeton: Princeton University Press, 2005.
PSM	*Powers of the Secular Modern: Talal Asad and His Interlocutors.* Edited by David Scott and Charles Hirschkind. Stanford: Stanford University Press, 2006.
RN	*Reinhold Niebuhr: His Religious, Social, and Political Thought.* Edited by Charles W. Kegley and Robert W. Bretall. New York: Macmillan, 1961.
RNCR	*Reinhold Niebuhr and Christian Realism.* Robin Lovin. Cambridge: Cambridge University Press, 1995.
RNPP	*Reinhold Niebuhr: Prophet to Politicians.* Ronald H. Stone. Nashville: Abingdon, 1972.
RNTPL	*Reinhold Niebuhr: Theologian of Public Life.* Reinhold Niebuhr. Edited by Larry Rasmussen. Minneapolis: Fortress, 1988.
RVMS	*Rival Views of Market Society and Other Recent Essays.* Albert O. Hirschman. Cambridge: Harvard University Press, 1992.
SDH	*The Self and the Dramas of History.* Reinhold Niebuhr. New York: Scribner's, 1955.
SNE	*The Structure of Nations and Empires.* Reinhold Niebuhr. New York: Scribner's, 1959.
WIANS	*Why I Am Not a Secularist.* William E. Connolly. Minneapolis: University of Minnesota Press, 1999.

1

Human Nature

The Transcendent and Finite Self

At the very heart of Niebuhr's theology and certainly his political and ethical thought is his view of human nature. That it is a powerful formulation goes without saying, having dominated Christian theological, ethical, and political thought in the United States throughout most of the twentieth century, not to mention its impact on secular thought and in other parts of the world. Niebuhr's view of the human condition was not original with him; he draws on resources such as Augustine and Kierkegaard, and he also apparently draws a good deal of his inspiration from the work of Emil Brunner.[1] Nevertheless, with his concept of human nature and his brilliant analysis of the human condition, Niebuhr addressed central issues facing the nation-state in the middle of the twentieth century; further, he used his views of human nature and analysis of the human condition as weapons

---

1. See Kegley and Bretall, *RN*, 32–33 where Emil Brunner states, "I was somewhat astonished to find no mention of the fact that in this work Reinhold Niebuhr had been strongly preoccupied with certain ideas which I had put forward in my book *Man in Revolt* in the year 1937, that is, four years before the publication of the first volume of Gifford Lectures." Later in the Kegley and Bretall volume Niebuhr acknowledges his need "to make amends for a grievous omission in my *The Nature and Destiny of Man, I.*" He states that he "profited greatly" from Brunner's analysis of the doctrine of sin in his *Man in Revolt*. But in studying the history of the doctrine Niebuhr states that he "lost sight of Brunner and did not refer to his work," though, as he confesses, "I had written appreciatively to him about the book. It was a grievous error not to acknowledge my debt to him" (431).

against a variety of political positions and postures of the time, which made an indelible and unique imprint.

I should say here just a word about where I'm heading with this chapter. I will challenge Niebuhr's existentialist view of the self, which he sees as primordial and universal. Against his view, I will contend that the human subject is socially formed, that in its historicity and sociolinguistic settings we find far more divergence in the makeup of the subject and a far more complex dynamic operative in the subjectivities of the self and its intersubjective relationships with others than Niebuhr allows. In other words, it is my intent to challenge Niebuhr's view of the self at its very core.

THE SELF AS SPIRIT AND NATURE

For Niebuhr human nature is a compound or composite of nature and spirit. This composite distinguishes human beings from all other creatures. Niebuhr states it succinctly: "The obvious fact is that man is a child of nature, subject to its vicissitudes, compelled by its necessities, driven by its impulses, and confined within the brevity of the years which nature permits its varied organic forms, allowing them some, but not too much, latitude. The other less obvious fact is that man is a spirit who stands outside of nature, life, himself, his reason and the world."[2]

As nature, human beings are limited. Our finitude marks our lives, our physical powers, our thought and reason, and, of course, our very years are limited by death. As nature or creature, Niebuhr includes those characteristics we share with other animals, such as our biological and organic makeup and our genetic inheritance. Our impulses, the urges and surges of our embodied character, factor into our nature as creature. We hunger and thirst, and as social creatures we require each other. We are driven in part by instinct and desire. Through evolution we emerge from simpler forms of biological life, but we are also a race born of family, clan, and tribe, having moved through history into wider communities of cities and nation-states, even civilizations.

Yet, if we are nature, and certainly on Niebuhr's view we are, we are also spirit, and by our spirit we transcend nature. We are the creature who can make an object of self, who is self-conscious, whose very freedom resides in that capacity to see ourselves, to see our limitations, to anticipate our very deaths and to know that there are limits to all we are, all we do, all

2. *NDM*1, 3.

we know, and all we can dream. This very self-consciousness is the source of our freedom, our capacity to imagine a different possibility, and the opportunity to decide upon a different path of action. More than this, the spirit is the transcendent unity of the self; it is "the ultimate freedom of the self over its inner divisions. . . . It is, in short, the self standing above its functions and capacities and yet proving its relation to them."[3]

Yet, as spirit and nature, humans are characterized by a profound tension between finitude and transcendence, such that an existential anxiety is generated in this tension. Because we are transcendent we can see that we are limited; because we can see we are limited, we know we will die. These characteristics set up an inevitable anxiety from which no one can escape, an anxiety that will characterize human existence throughout all of life in every time and in every place. This anxiety must be distinguished from fear because fear has an object. In fear we are afraid of something. Anxiety, however, has no object; it arises from the self-consciousness of human freedom where one can know the limitations of existence. Thus human freedom is always an anxious freedom.[4]

It is this anxiety that is the occasion of sin and the source of temptation to sin. It is important to understand that anxiety does not *cause* sin, but rather is the *occasion* of sin. It is in this anxiety that one is tempted to escape from existence, an escape that occurs in basically two ways. The first is a flight into self-elevation, into pride or arrogance, an attempt to relieve anxiety by some denial of finitude.[5] The subtleties of this are enormous. They can take the form of an arrogance about one's strength, one's knowledge or intelligence, one's sexual prowess or athletic ability, one's good looks, point of view, business acumen, spiritual awareness, or courage—even arrogance about one's humility! It is the sin of overreach.

The other direction of escape from anxiety is that of finitude. This is the direction of self-loss, of passivity, of denial of one's human freedom and capacity. It is the sin of sensuality, the attempt to be nothing more than an animal. It is losing the self in its passions, its impulses, its compulsions, its pleasures, and its irrationalities. It is abandonment of the freedom of the self. It is failure of nerve, the loss of meaning beyond the placation of the energies of the dimension of nature in the self; it is the sin of underreach.[6]

3. *SDH*, 41.
4. *NDM*2, 178–86.
5. Ibid., 186–203.
6. See *NDM*2, 228–40, *MNHC*, 118.

In both arrogance and sensuality there is a participation of the one in the other—that is, the turn to sensuality is its own kind of arrogance because the self diverts itself from its status before God, a turning away from its vocation and destiny in God. In its flights of self-elevation and arrogance, there is a self-loss by the denial of the finite dimensions of the self, a denial of its creaturely status before God, and hence an underreach. The subtleties of this interpenetration of arrogance and sensuality are immense and when given careful attention open up analytically the genius and, perhaps, the most profound insight of the Niebuhrian position. Certainly, it moves away from the moralizing of pride and sensuality in some simplistic way that ignores the existential dynamics of the self, so understood, with all its complexity and concreteness.[7]

There is no escape by the self from this existential condition. Niebuhr uses language like "absolute," "immutable," "the primordial structure" in discussing the nature of the self.[8] He clearly understands that there are always "historically contingent elements" and "new emergents in the human situation"; nevertheless, the "immutable structure" of human nature resides in all cultures and throughout human history. Again, "it belongs to the freedom of man to create new configurations of freedom and necessity," but this primordial structure remains.[9] "There is not much that is absolutely immutable in the structure of human nature except it's animal basis, man's freedom to transmute this nature in varying degrees, and the unity of the natural and the spiritual and all the various transmutations and transfigurations of the original 'nature.'" In the discussions I report in this paragraph Niebuhr is speaking against modern views, which tend to obscure this existential condition by invoking some "laws of nature," or some "natural" categories understood as "primordial," or in some incorporation "into a general norm." But Niebuhr is adamant that human nature itself is immutable; only its particular historic expressions can be changed.[10]

Furthermore, these dynamics of the self are compounded in social life. It is not only that the collective arrogance of individuals can be conjoined in the idolatries and certitudes of social movements, institutions, societies, and especially nation-states, but also that even the capacities of the self for self-giving and sacrifice—including the ultimate sacrifice of life itself—can

---

7. *NDM2*, esp. 233f., 235–40.
8. *FH*, 179, 180–81, 183.
9. Ibid., 179.
10. *FH*, 183.

serve the most wicked aims and ambitions of human group life.[11] Niebuhr states that "the most obvious forms of idolatry" are found in "the life of a tribe or nation" where these "natural historical vitalities" become the center of meaning and value. But idolatry takes more "covert forms" when a penultimate "principle of coherence and meaning" is understood in ultimate terms.[12]

By way of illustration of Niebuhr's point, I think of soldiers who will crawl across an open field while under heavy fire and give their lives to grenade a machine gun nest, and yet who do so in behalf of the indefensible imperialistic ambitions of their nation. But we can find endless illustrations of the sacrificial giving of the self to the egoistic aims of human collectives. I think of professionals in think tanks who give unstintingly of their time, who devote themselves fully to the organization's work, who sacrifice their lives with their families, and who narrow the very richness of their own personalities in pursuit of findings and discourses that serve only the most narrow interests of the corporations or organizations that fund them. Or I think of churches where a few individuals give themselves up selflessly to serve the self-satisfied aims of a misguided congregation in a largely abject dismissal of the gospel of Christ.

VITALITY AND FORM IN THE SELF

As we have seen, a human being is a creature who lives "at the juncture of nature and spirit," to quote Niebuhr.[13] But there is one further twofold distinction required to grasp more fully Niebuhr's basic understanding of human nature: the role of vitality and form. These "two aspects of creation" can be found in all creatures and "express an exuberant vitality within the limits of certain unities, orders and forms." Human existence, however, must be distinguished from other creatures because of its participation in creation not only as nature but as spirit. Within certain bounds, humans can break the forms nature takes and bring about "new configurations of vitality." Humans in their transcendent freedom can disrupt "the established forms and unities of vitality" as found in nature and in other creatures.[14] To grasp Niebuhr's view here I find it helpful to think in terms of a matrix with

11. *MMIS*, 92–95.
12. *NDM*1, 165.
13. Ibid., 231.
14. Ibid., 26.

form and vitality on one axis and spirit and nature on the other. This matrix is then made up of four cells: spirit/form, spirit/vitality, nature/form, and nature/vitality.[15]

As can be seen in this matrix, Niebuhr's understanding is that vitality and form characterize not only nature but spirit as well in human beings. We cannot separate nature in human beings as the realm of energies and vitalities from form and its ordering capacities. Our bodies and our animal natures cannot be reduced to urges, impulses, and appetites alone. These energies do not come without forms of their own. They are not ordered by spirit or by reason and culture alone, but rather are constituted by certain limits, regulations, and arrangements that, in part, structure their dynamics. We share with the creaturely world biological and sociobiological characteristics: our sexuality, requisites of shelter, nutritional and health requirements, the need for security and protection, the necessary sociality of family, and the natural cohesion of basic community.

At the same time, we are spirit, possessing the vitalities of this dimension of the self in imagination, in the dynamics of reason itself, and in yearnings issuing forth from a transcendent freedom that can gaze upon itself, upon the world and its history, and see new possibilities, dream dreams, and invest the world with vision. But spirit also has form-creating capacities in its use of reason to bring order to thought and its bringing of coherence and direction to social, political, and economic affairs. It is expressed in craft, art, and in ordinary life. It is the planning, organizing, and rational use of space and temporality. It is that human capacity, within limits, to give shape to the environment around us.

But no impulse of nature acts alone, and no striving for rationality, order, and coherence stands free of its base in the vitalities of nature. The actor in the drama of history is the self compounded of nature and spirit with each of these constituted of vitality and form and with all of these dimensions interfused and conjoined in the self.

Niebuhr notes that the four factors of the vitality and form of nature and spirit are profoundly engaged in both human creativity and destructiveness. While the vitality and form of nature may be the more passive

---

15. Niebuhr proposes "four terms" required for the consideration of vitality and form: "(1) the vitality of nature (its impulses and drives); (2) the forms and unities of nature, that is, the determinations of instinct, and the forms of natural cohesion and natural differentiation; (3) the freedom of spirit to transcend natural forms within limits and to direct and redirect the vitalities; (4) and finally the forming capacity of spirit, its ability to create a new realm of coherence and order." Ibid., 27.

resources in contrast to "active agents" in human creativity and destructiveness, they must not be ignored. Indeed, basic to Niebuhr's criticism of modern culture is the way in which one of these factors, as understood by modern culture, becomes "the principle of interpretation of the whole." For example, the rationalists understand the world too much in terms of form and spirit, while the romanticists see things too much in terms of nature and vitality. Each and all of these four factors are central to a more compelling interpretation of the world and of contemporary life.[16]

Much more can, of course, be said about Niebuhr's understanding of human nature, but this is enough to give us a basic grasp of his view for my purposes. My intention is to raise question with this very procedure of positing a view of the nature of the self. More specifically, I will lay out a view of the social formation of the human subject that in its historicity and sociolinguistic settings offers a far more plural and relative view and calls into question Niebuhr's claim that the self is a composite of spirit and nature characterized by the dynamics detailed in his argument.

A CRITIQUE OF NIEBUHR'S VIEW OF HUMAN NATURE

Anthropologist Saba Mahmood, in her brilliant study of the women's mosque movement in Cairo, proposes an approach to the person as subject with which I will address the self as understood by Reinhold Niebuhr. It is the first move in my attempt to call Niebuhr's view of human nature into question. I want to suggest that the self or subject is far more constituted than it is constituting, and that the shape of the subject is far more diverse than Niebuhr's view. One may wonder how anyone can call into question the self's capacity to make an object of itself through its self-consciousness, and one may wonder how one can doubt that the self is finite. These things seem self-evident, and in one sense they are. Nevertheless, I contend that Mahmood provides a cogent alternative to this Niebuhrian view.

Mahmood's research focuses on a grassroots piety and moral reform movement in three mosques in Cairo—one that is upper middle class, another that is middle class, and a third that is lower class. Such movements are often seen as having no impact on political realities, but Mahmood counters this view by demonstrating how ethics and politics are inextricably bound up together in this movement.

16. Ibid.

Mahmood begins by refusing the assumption that a given culture at a given time has "a homogeneous notion of the self." That is, her inquiry rejects the notion that a self with "an individuated consciousness" somehow precedes and uses various bodily practices to acquire a cultural particularity. Indeed, as we shall see, the self—or, actually, the subject for Mahmood—emerges from these linguistic and bodily practices rather than precedes them.

Her work, moreover, demonstrates that *different* and multiple configurations of personhood reside in the *same* culture and in the *same* historical time ("temporality"). These different, simultaneously existing configurations of personhood are the products of what she calls "a specific discursive formation" or, in other words, a form of life in a given time and place with its particular linguistic and material practices.[17] According to Mahmood, "there is no single conception of the self that corresponds to the discursive practices of a given culture." Rather, a diversity of conceptions of the self—and even conflicted and conflicting conceptions thereof—can occupy a specific culture, with the diversities and tensions within and between differently configured "selves" dependent upon what is understood to be the truth in a given form of life, that is, the reigning view of what can be said and heard as true in a given time and place.[18]

---

17. *PP*, 121.

18. Ibid., 121 n. 4. Mahmood is working here with Foucault's concept of discourse and truth. His concept is quite complex. For now, five aspects of this concept should be delineated. First, discourse is quite material for Foucault; it does not focus on intention or on subjective consciousness. Rather it centers on what people say, write, and argue about, and discourse addresses what people know in these terms. Second, Foucault deals with discourse in terms of use, not meaning; so his attention is addressed to discursive practices as well as to non-discursive practices. Third, by working with the use of concepts, Foucault is able to analyze rules that determine the forms discursive rationality takes that operate below the level of intentions or even the content or themes of discourse. These rules are not universals; they change over time, they vary, and they are found in very different concepts, theoretical formulations, and focuses of study. Fourth, Foucault develops a relationship between discourse and truth quite different from that of the correspondence theory of truth, which argues for truth as a match between certain discursive claims and the state of affairs that actually exists in some metaphysical or ultimate sense. For Foucault "truth is a thing of this world"; truth is understood as intelligibility between a discursive formation and a specific form of life. That is, truth has to do with what can actually be said and done with credibility in a given time and place. Further, Foucault understands truth as "the ensemble of rules" by which truth and falsity are separated, with quite specific effects of power connected to the former. As understood by Foucault truth is "a system of ordered procedures for the production, regulation, distribution, circulation and operation of statements." *P/K*, 132. In these procedures

Mahmood focuses on "the empirical character of bodily practices" as the place where particular conceptions of the self are formed. For example, the ways in which interiority and exteriority are conceptualized and articulated develop different understandings of the self and its relationship to others. Mahmood claims that bodily practices develop "the architecture of the self" through the immanent forms these practices embody. Hence Mahmood's conception of self is one in which the self "becomes" via practices—that is, it does not exist ontologically like Niebuhr's self (on the basis of which he could elaborate a universal and unchangeable human nature). Mahmood's self is one that comes into being as it is exercised. She observes that her conception of the self reverses the typical "routing from interiority to exteriority" where the movement is one in which the unconscious expresses itself in bodily forms.[19] Indebted here both to Pierre Hadot and Michel Foucault, she understands such bodily practices to be physical, discursive, or intuitive, yet in any modality characterized by the intent to modify or to transform the person performing them.

What is impressive analytically in this exposition of the self, Mahmood asserts, is "the *work* bodily practices perform in crafting a subject—rather than the *meanings* they signify."[20] Further, she states, "Bodily behavior does not simply stand in a relationship of meaning to self and society, but it also endows itself with certain kinds of capacities that provide the substance from which the world is acted upon."[21] Through practices the self is shaped and cultivated.[22] Note, for example, the difference here between freedom as choice and freedom as capacity. When it comes to playing the piano I have, in human terms, endless choices, because I can hardly play the piano at all. "All of my options are open," to use a popular expression. My friend Gene Lowry is an excellent jazz pianist. He has freedom in the sense of a capacity

---

truth and power are tied together in "a circular relation" so that power systems "produce and sustain" truth while truth induces certain effects of power and extends them. P/K, 133. By such operations a regime of truth comes to be. Finally, in his work on discourse Foucault typically gives attention to the normal, the typical, the conventional; that is, he does not usually attend to crises, or exceptional cases, but rather to the typical, ongoing operations of discourse in a form of life in a given time and place.

19. Ibid., 121–22.

20. Ibid., 122. Mahmood's italics.

21. Ibid., 27.

22. One of the problems here is that the focus on meaning makes subjectivity too important in the larger context of behavior by conceding too much explanatory power to its role. See Asad, "Trouble with Thinking," 272f.

not only to play any tune someone can whistle or sing or play for him, but he can then also turn it into a fine jazz rendition. He has the freedom of a trained and skilled capaciousness in the rich art and craft of the piano. He has the freedom of a virtuoso; I have the freedom of severely limited choices. It is in the former sense that Mahmood discusses the capacities cultivated in the subject by the practices of a discursive formation. It is in this sense that the subject takes on agency.

It needs to be understood here that Mahmood is working with Foucault's concept of power, which stands sharply against conceptions of power as either oppression or repression taken alone. Foucault refutes the model of power in which it is viewed as a possession of either individuals or ruling agents. Power is not exercised *over* others to suppress their wills or desires in order to enforce the power-wielder's own. In such a model, power is always power over others. For Foucault, power is "a strategic relation of force that permeates life and is *productive* of new forms of desires, objects, relations, and discourses" (emphasis added). Power doesn't just suppress, it produces. Understood this way, the subject as "a form of individuated consciousness" does not exist prior to power relations, but, indeed, is produced and constituted *through* these relations. The subject is the *result* of power rather than the *wielder* thereof in this conception. Foucault calls this "the paradox of subjectivation," meaning by this that the very procedures and circumstances that subordinate a subject are, at the same time, the very means by which that subject is formed in both identity and agency.[23]

The point of this for Mahmood is that the very capacities of a subject—the endowments that constitute the means of agency for the subject—are not the leftovers of some essential, "dominated self" that was "there" prior to the dynamics of power and that managed to hold out in the face of them. Instead, the capacities of a subject (in her case, the mosque women) are the *product* of those relations of power.[24] It should be noted in this regard that Mahmood does not attempt to offer a theory of agency, but rather observes that agency must be examined by "the grammar of concepts within which it resides." She therefore doesn't define human agency in general. Her wont is to leave the definition of agency open and to let definitions come forth from the specific networks of language, practices, and institutions whereby

---

23. Foucault, *P/K*, 87–102, 183–93, 198–202; Foucault, *FR*, 11, 173–78.
24. Mahmood, *PP*, 17.

the avenues by which people relate to each other, to objects, and to the self are defined and made available.[25]

As indicated, Mahmood works with Foucault's understanding of power as a productive relation of force. The concept of force is crucial here, and by the word *force* Foucault means that power is always bound up with the body and its energies. The body has its own energies, and these energies constitute, in part, what Foucault means by force. At the same time, the body must be subjected into "a useful force" if it is to be "productive," that is, the body is subjected to a wide range of technologies and practices. This subjection can occur through violence, ideology, and by the direct countering of one physical force by another. Subjection also can involve highly computed, utilitarian considered, technical processes, or it can also be quite subtle, not making use of violent coercion or terror (even though it may still be physical).

Force also refers to a "knowledge of the body," in Foucault's use of the term. This kind of knowledge is not precisely identical with that of disciplines like biology or medicine. Rather, this kind of knowledge of the body shapes people's understandings throughout a form of life. It involves procedures and skills to carry them out. It includes things as concrete as the procedures and skills of parenting a child, of knowing how to work in a gang, of how to conduct meetings, of how to relate to other people appropriately in different social settings, and so on. The skilled use of practices in various settings can marshal unity and a willingness to work together. Such procedures may not involve coercion—although manipulation cannot be ruled out—but these procedures certainly require a skilled understanding of how bodies/people work in relationship to each other and the kind of energies that such relationships generate. Further, these kinds of procedures do require a mastery of certain kinds of forces for Foucault, but these go beyond simply a conquest of them.

The knowledge of the body in this sense constitutes a dimension of what Foucault calls "the political technology of the body." Moreover, this kind of technology is widely spread and not usually stated in a kind of "continuous systematic discourse," when considered, for example, in terms of the expansive uses of coming to consensus in a broad range of social relationships in ordinary life that go beyond those in educational settings or other more formal places. Foucault speaks of this technology as typically "a multiform instrumentation," suggesting that these practices cannot

---

25. Ibid., 34. She is working here with Asad, *FS*, 78.

be ascribed to a specific institution, not even to the apparatus of the state or the economy. Rather, on Foucault's view, these larger apparatuses typically make use of "a micro-physics of power"—operating in a host of ways all across a society, its institutions, and its interpersonal relations—whose operations occur in between the workings of these apparatuses and people's bodies.

Further, this power that subjectivates the body cannot be possessed like a property, but rather is to be understood as "a strategy," so that the outcomes of domination are not ascribed to "appropriation" but to "dispositions, maneuvers, tactics, techniques, functionings . . ." So, to continue the example of learning to work in a gang, certain dispositions are formed in groups, specific maneuvers of communication are developed, particular tactics and techniques of listening, restatement, clarifying difference, and searching for agreement not only come into play but shape the people engaged in these procedures. We may not think of domination in these terms because I have chosen a more "positive" example, but, for Foucault, domination is constituted of "a network of relations" ever "in tension," ever mobile and active, "rather than a privilege that one might possess." It is to be taken more as a constant struggle, and not "a contract regulating a transaction or the conquest of a territory."

Hence, on my reading of Foucault, force is constituted of the energies of the body, but of those energies in a host of relational potencies as well, of discourses and practices of domination in a given time and place, a domination that not only subjectifies the body but also produces its capacity to be an agent.[26] In Foucault's view, therefore, domination and production go hand in hand: power dominates as part of its process of production of certain kinds of subjects and agencies that said subjects enact, take on, and become. Power dominates, but it is also productive.

Obviously influenced by Michel Foucault, Mahmood opposes the notion of "a voluntaristic, autonomous subject" who constitutes the self in the acquiring of cultural and historical characteristics, so that to the preexisting self, various cultural "stuff" is added, thus resulting in a particular subjectivity. In contrast, her view approaches the subject as constituted all the way down within the frameworks of "a historically specific set of formative practices and moral injunctions." In other words, Mahmood does not presume that there is any preexisting, existential, or essential self to add "cultural stuff" to. Any self that exists, she argues, is one that is formed *in*

---

26. Foucault, *DP*, 25–26.

culture—in, through, and by practices of thinking and acting. Foucault's name for this process of self-formation is "modes of subjectivation"—that is, modes of becoming and/or producing subjectivity.

Subjectivity understood in this way is *not* a personal arena of cultivation by the self. Subjectivity is the result of what Foucault calls a "modality of power" that calls or prompts the subject to formation in the terms of its teaching. That is, the self is formed—called or practiced into being—within an arena that is limited, and these processes through which the self is formed/practiced into existence are power at work. The self is formed in and through the dynamics of power. Moral subjectivation, then, concerns models for conduct that cultivate certain relations of the self *with* itself—forms of reflection, self-knowledge, and corrective self-examination—whose purpose is to transform the subject in accord with the aims of a tradition understood as a form of life with its practices of acting and thinking.[27]

Mahmood addresses two possible objections to her view of subjectivation. The first objection is to the claim of the self as "an effect of power." This objection presumes a self as an *agent* of power or a self-conscious agent who is self-constituting in the sense of enacting one's will and asserting agency against structural forces. Mahmood states flatly that this perception is erroneous. In her research on the activities of the mosque movement women she found them to be "products of authoritative discursive traditions whose logic and power exceeds the consciousness of the subjects they enable." The agency she examines with the mosque movement women is not the kind of agency *possessed* by the women themselves as something they *have* as a result of tapping into some universal, existential "fund" called "agency" to which they can avail themselves. Rather, Mahmood argues that their agency is better understood as "a product of the historically contingent discursive traditions in which they are located." In the case of the mosque women the individual is not the expression of some essential, universal self, but rather a woman who is formed in the discourses and practices of the tradition of Islam she enacts. Referring again to Foucault, Mahmood argues that the self-reflexivity of the mosque movement women is not a universal human attribute but rather is a *specific* type of relationship to oneself that, at its most basic level, is constituted by "the practices of subjectivation through which the individual is produced."[28] In short, it is an agency that is specific

27. Ibid., 28.
28. Mahmood, *PP*, 32.

and particular, allowing them to be and do certain things in certain contexts because of the specific type of people they are. This is not agency *in general*—freedom to do anything—but agency *in particular*—the ability to pursue certain types of actions and to inhabit certain types of subjectivities in the particular circumstances of that form of life.

The other objection to Mahmood's view of "agency as ethical self-formation" is that it forsakes politics. This charge relates to a prominent understanding of the modern nation-state in which the state remains uncommitted to any moral goods but rather is to establish and sustain human rights, with morality taking up residence in the private, peripheral sphere of the society and therefore without a central role in the public square. Mahmood notes that this objection is reminiscent of an enduring distinction within liberal political theory between the private and the public, with ethics and morality inhabiting the former and politics the latter. Such a distinction is problematic, according to Mahmood, for a number of reasons. For one, there is disagreement within liberal thought itself about "the proper role of ethics and virtue."[29] Indeed, we have already seen that Niebuhr is not only a political realist but a moral and theological one as well, suggesting that this problematic distinction does not necessarily characterize all realist thought, and clearly indicating a role for ethics and theology in politics on Niebuhr's view.

Further, this compartmentalization of the ethical and the political faces additional difficulties when one contemplates what has become virtually a commonplace in the scholarly world today. According to Mahmood, this commonplace maintains that every type of politics has its own specific "kind of subject that is produced through a range of disciplinary practices that are at the core of the regulative apparatus of any modern political arrangement." She then raises a question that must be put to Niebuhr: "How does a particular conception of the self require and presuppose different kinds of political commitments?" Or in other words, what is the relationship between a given political imaginary and the kind of subject that it not only enjoins, but normatively takes for granted?[30] Her conclusion on this point is that "the self is socially and discursively produced, an *effect* of operations of power rather than the *progenitor* of these operations." If the self is an effect of power, then the appropriate object of study actually is not "the personal preferences and proclivities of the *individual*." Instead, the

29. Ibid.
30. Ibid., 33.

appropriate object of study is "the historically contingent arrangements of power" whereby the normative subject of a specific political imaginary is constituted.[31] That is, rather than hone in on the dynamics of the individual self in order to understand the machinations of politics, focus instead on the discourses and practices of power and the way they function to produce subjects and intersubjective relations. The relations of power, of force, produce the subject, not the other way around.

MAHMOOD AND NIEBUHR

At this point let us return to Reinhold Niebuhr and examine his understanding of human nature in the light of Mahmood's constituted subject. First, it needs to be said that Niebuhr does not fall under some of the characteristics Mahmood develops in her characterization of a constituting self—for example, the autonomous self, which Niebuhr explicitly rejects.[32] Moreover, he is sensitive to the ways in which the self is shaped by culture and history.[33] Niebuhr is also critical of the arguments of liberal thinkers such as Hobbes and Locke in their discussions of humans living in a state of nature prior to the contractual obligations of the state, which place him in some tension with these early liberal thinkers.[34]

At the same time, Niebuhr does hold to a view of human nature, a view of the self, that is primordial and universal. While he does not hold to an autonomous self, he certainly does hold to an individuating one in Mahmood's terms. This existential structure of the self, as Niebuhr conceives of it, operates in all times and places, in all cultures and all of human history. In this sense it is existentially "prior" to personal and human life; it is a constituting self. While Niebuhr can indeed argue against a homogeneous notion of the self, in acknowledging that human nature can take on a host of historical and cultural characteristics, there is no sense in which his self can lose this fundamental human nature which operates with its dynamic of anxious freedom in any and all circumstances. Certainly there is plurality in the cultural forms and historicity of the self in Niebuhr's view, but not in its fundamental human nature, which, he is adamant, remains everywhere and at all times the same.

31. Ibid.
32. *NDM*1, 59–61.
33. *CLCD*, 50f.
34. *NDM*2, 95.

Human Nature, Interest, and Power

NIEBUHR'S HISTORY OF INDIVIDUALITY

It is noteworthy at this point that Niebuhr does address the historicity of the concept of individuality. After introducing individuality as "the product of spirit as well as of nature," Niebuhr argues that "nature supplies particularity but the freedom of the spirit is the cause of real individuality." He further indicates that "human consciousness" not only "transcends natural process," it also "transcends itself." By this dynamic the self accrues its potential for the unlimited "variations and elaboration of human capacities" that distinguish human history. In fact, Niebuhr has such confidence in the human capacity for self-transcendence that he argues, "To a certain degree man is free to reject one environment for another. If he dislikes the spiritual environment of the twentieth century *he may consciously choose to live by the patterns of the thirteenth century*."[35] (Surely, upon further reflection, Niebuhr might wince at having made such a claim.)

He then addresses the historical emergence of "the Renaissance doctrine of individuality," a doctrine, says Niebuhr, founded in human greatness and in the uniqueness of the individual, especially in its freedom and the freedom of the will. Niebuhr reports that the doctrine is influenced by "various philosophical and theological ideas" but argues that its cultural roots are those of Christianity. Raising the question of why such a doctrine came to expression when it did and then why it "dominated the culture of modernity" until more recent times, Niebuhr answers that the source of the doctrine of individuality must be understood in light of several social antecedents—namely, the emergence of the commercial world and its bourgeois classes.[36] More specifically, he argues that "the Italian city states were the seed-plot of bourgeois culture." While other parts of Europe were still under the aegis of land-holding aristocrats, the emerging business classes of the Italian cities had the chance to form their own culture. These processes of formation can be understood to foreshadow "the culture of the Enlightenment," which marked "the triumph of the business man" in all of Europe.[37] In fact, Niebuhr names the characteristics of the form of economic power that gives rise to the bourgeois classes—namely, "individual initiative," "resourcefulness," "dynamic ... social relationships," and a sense of "history as a realm of human decisions." These characteristics stand

---

35. *ND*1, 55-56. Italics mine.
36. Ibid., 65.
37. Ibid.

in sharp contrast to the characteristics of previous social arrangements, with their more static social relationships that were defined by ascribed rather than achieved status and a view of history as "inexorable destiny." The emergent bourgeois classes understood nature not as "the master of the human will" but in instrumental terms, as a wealth of many different resources humans can harness and use. With the development of science, a new sense of human mastery over nature eventually provided new energy to the notion of human self-sufficiency.[38]

Niebuhr notes that these shifts spelled a growing estimate of human powers and their capacity to impact history and nature, and he claims that these sensibilities "subtly merged" with Christian views of the importance of each individual in the eyes of God, especially in a "this-worldly version of the latter." Here Niebuhr follows the work of Max Weber, who maintained that the otherworldly asceticism of at least some parts of Christianity became a this-worldly asceticism of rational economic activity in the nascent years of capitalism. Niebuhr concurs with Weber that this influence of Christianity and capitalism came primarily from Protestantism, and Niebuhr, taking his cue from Weber, asserts that this is proved by the fact that capitalism emerged in the Protestant nations and not in Catholic countries or those that were non-Christian.

He suggests that further proof is proffered by "the bewildering complexity of interactions" that occurred between the religious individualism of Protestantism and that of the secular individualism of bourgeois culture.[39] Niebuhr believes that the "modern individual" would not have come to be *except* in a Christian culture. Nevertheless, he laments that the development of the modern individual also undid what he calls "the Christian basis of individuality"—namely, the crucial notion that humans are both spirit and nature and that without the particularity of the body the individual is "easily lost in the universality of divine spirit, in the undifferentiated being of eternity."[40]

From this point on in the text, Niebuhr continues an analysis of modern commercial industrialization and its impact on individuals.[41] It is not necessary to continue this outline of the historical developments Niebuhr traces in order to raise my question: how is it possible for such a process

38. Ibid., 66.
39. Ibid.
40. Ibid., 63f.
41. Ibid., 66f.

of unfolding individuality to occur—with its individualism, with its formations of initiative, resourcefulness, and dynamic sociality, and with a view of history as the theater of human action and decision—without major shifts in the subjectivities of the people undergoing such massive, thoroughgoing change?

Niebuhr typically has an extraordinarily keen sense of the historical *contingency* of human life, with all its vicissitudes, ambiguities, and fragmentation, and his report of the history of individuality certainly conveys something of each of these. Given this, why does a specific understanding of human nature escape such contingency? On the one hand, I suspect Niebuhr makes this exception because he sees transcendence and finitude as inexorable dimensions of the self and as ever present in human life. While these dynamics can take on an individuality (as in the modern period), these dynamics remain basically unchanged, simply finding new forms in which those dynamics are expressed.

Yet, on the other hand, I want to press the question of whether it is the case that the dynamics of human nature really remain basically unchanged. In fact, I wonder if this is true even in Niebuhr's own writing. To explore this question, I will treat the dynamics of transcendence and finitude in Niebuhr's view of human nature as concepts, and as such I will examine them in terms of the variations of the uses of the concepts themselves. First, I begin with transcendence.

It is noteworthy again that Niebuhr attributes to Christianity responsibility for what he calls "a heightened sense of individuality." The ultimate claim of God on human life provides a powerful rationale for the transcendability of tribal customs, various "rational rules of conduct, and all general and abstract norms of behavior." Niebuhr makes the claim that "during the whole period of medieval Catholicism Christian individuality never came to a consistent expression" because *"social complexity had not yet forced the full emergence of individual consciousness."*[42] The social conditions, in other words, were not favorable for the full expression of "Christian individuality."

Not only were the social conditions not favorable, Niebuhr further claims that Catholicism actually *forestalled* "the emergence of a high sense of individuality," a result, in part, of its combination of Greek rationalism and natural law, and in part its own authoritarianism. Niebuhr states flatly, "Since the will of God which transcended all rational abstractions was

---

42. Ibid., 59. Italics mine.

nevertheless completely interpreted by an historic institution, involving casuistic applications of general norms to specific situations, the individual always remained conscious of the general categories, social, moral and political of which he was an exemplar. *He never expressed himself fully as an individual.*"[43] In Niebuhr's formation, to be/become/exist as an individual required the transcendence of these social, economic, political, and religious factors so that the individual *qua* individual could emerge. Christianity in its Catholic form was not capable of supporting an individual thus constituted.

At this point, I will not challenge Niebuhr's overly generalized view of the medieval world or his uncharitable anti-Catholicism. Instead, I am most interested to highlight that his argument here indicates that *transcendence itself is a mobile concept.* In Niebuhr's usage, transcendence is, apparently, affected by a host of factors—economic, social, religious, and scientific factors, among others. Niebuhr tells us explicitly that the full emergence of individuality was attended by social complexity and that no one expressed herself or himself fully as an individual before the modern period.

I contend that one simply cannot argue for a uniform notion of consciousness or self-consciousness when explored in the contingencies, ambiguities, and fragmentations of history. I wonder, for example, what happens with people who think far more relationally than they do individualistically, particularly people in some of the traditional medieval contexts to which Niebuhr refers. Does the practice of the self in making an object of itself operate in Niebuhrian terms, or must one not explore self-reflexivity in specific historical contexts and raise question with what these dynamics are? When the focus of self-consciousness is far more powerfully communal than individual, will self-reflexivity not be different? What happens to the dynamics of the self (really the subject) when one reads carefully the impact of social, economic, political, religious, and cultural influences on humans such as Niebuhr describes?

Turning to the concept of finitude, Niebuhr was, of course, correct to observe and take seriously that human beings are limited in a host of ways—in physical and mental ability, for example, or in length of life. Yet I question Niebuhr's ahistorical and static conception of finitude much the way I have just questioned his ahistorical conception of transcendence. This leads me to questions regarding the *specific* character of limits as found in subjects in *particular* forms of life. In a sense, perhaps no limitation is

---

43. Ibid. Italics mine.

clearer than death. Yet death is understood in so many ways across different forms of life and, for that matter, within forms of life. Religious extremists will see death quite differently from most others if they believe that they will suddenly find themselves in a paradise filled with pleasure and plenty immediately after an act of violence that kills them and many others. Or, in a highly individualized culture based in the discourses and practices of achieved status, the concepts of limits will take on a radically different subjective form than it will among those in cultures with an ascribed status. My point is that both concepts of reflexivity and limits take on variable usages in different subjects in and within different forms of life in given times and places.

It is also important to see that there are a good many other dynamics in the subject, which are not covered by the basic concepts of Niebuhr's view. A simple question clarifies my concern: If, for Niebuhr, the entire dynamic of human nature can be characterized by the tension between transcendence and finitude, and the anxiety to which this fundamentally irresolvable tension gives rise, what gets ignored? I press this question because all-encompassing binary opposites are notorious for their capacity to hijack a range of matters elided by such linguistic dichotomies. What keeps the framework Niebuhr proposes from functioning as an imperial set of concepts that obscures or overlooks or gets readily transmuted into Niebuhr's categories? I think here of other concepts/practices that don't clearly fit anywhere in this binary that yet can be trenchantly proffered in describing the self. In what follows I explore the phenomenology of sin, the self-conscious self, various practices of introspection, and layers of subjectivity and intersubjectivity in the subject. I begin with the complex weave of the phenomenology of sin.

THE COMPLEX WEAVE OF THE PHENOMENOLOGY OF SIN

In *The Ways of Judgment* Oliver O'Donovan criticizes Niebuhr from the perspective of Augustine on the matter of pride. According to O'Donovan, Augustine privileged sin as pride and analyzed it in terms of two poles: a protological pole where all sin derives from "an original act of pride," and a historical pole where pride takes on a paradigmatic embodiment "in the ambitions of political empire."[44] O'Donovan suggests that this Augustinian

44. As I indicate above, Niebuhr also addresses sin as sensuality, as under reach, but

polarity became for Niebuhr a compelling way to address the various totalitarian regimes and intellectual tendencies that emerged in the mid-twentieth century. Niebuhr saw human rebellion against God and its idolatrous usurpation as the fundamental religious expression of sin. In the arena of morality and social life sin finds expression in injustice. The self-centered ego deceives itself and gives itself over to pride and will to power, attempting to bring others under its control, which results in the injustice of imbalances of power. Niebuhr, alert to the totalitarianisms of his times, found that such a view of sin and injustice required the checks and balances of a democratic order. Furthermore, such a view found an appropriate place in a "democratic tradition" begun in the seventeenth century that attempted to control the tyrannies of absolute monarchs and their efforts at absolute rule.[45]

Yet, O'Donovan finds difficulties with Niebuhr's connection of Augustine's view of pride to a twentieth-century democratic approach. The difficulty arises both on what O'Donovan calls the protological and the historical poles. First, on Augustine's account of the protological pole, pride is not the single factor, but rather "a thread within a complex weave," argues O'Donovan. The arrogance of Satan was not aimed "downward against subordinates, but upward against God."[46] Hence, the problem of pride had more to do with envy than with tyranny. On O'Donovan's view, the core of sin is composed of narcissism rather than pride or envy as such.

Second, when Augustine examines the sin of Adam and Eve, "the model of open-eyed defiance will not fit." This kind of rebellion required an angel, the only creature who could so stand before God. By contrast, human sin is ever caught up in "epistemological ambiguity," that is, it is always *mediated* and therefore different from angelic sin. Human sin is social, not solitary; it is aroused by "false communications" that cloak the defiant work of the will.

Third, for Augustine the progeny of Adam and Eve take on yet another difference "in that the 'wound' of human nature is always presupposed as a constraining necessity, manifest in the passionate resistance of carnal instinct to the control of human reason." Thus, on the protological

---

this receives far less attention in his work than does pride or arrogance. In fact, Langdon Gilkey sees Niebuhr's work on sin as sensuality "not so brilliantly argued" and it does not "function as importantly either in his own view or in subsequent theological discussion." Gilkey, *ON*, 141 n. 15.

45. *Ways of Judgment*, 78–79.
46. Ibid.

pole of Augustine's understanding of sin, pride is only *one* of the themes that contributes to "a psychological spectrum" wherein deception, shortsightedness, impotence, and envy all play significant roles. On this basis, O'Donovan characterizes the difference between Augustine and Niebuhr as one in which "will" is primary for Niebuhr, while love is primary for Augustine. Niebuhr's language of "will" centers attention on "sheer choice" and focuses everything on the question of who dominates whom. Augustine's language of love enters into the question of "motivational structure" and the place of perception and misperception therein.[47]

Turning to the historical pole, the issue of pride in Augustine continues to be quite complex. The imperial self-elevation of Rome is the consequence of the illusions of polytheism, a deception brought on Rome by demons, but these illusions are actively joined in by the populace, a consequence that comes naturally with empire, according to Augustine, along with bondage to the sensual as, in Augustine's words, "its natural corollary." The point is that the social sin of Rome cannot be reduced to one of unchecked power. The "will to power" does not encompass the lust for ascendancy that characterized Rome. Rather, Rome was consumed by its seeking of status before others, by its hunger for admiration. There were, of course, times of brutality and conquest by Rome over others, but O'Donovan argues that "its pride was the pride of a civilization, rather than the pride of an oppression." Even the ambition that fueled its greatest accomplishments—its ambition as benefactor—came from "the glory of 'sparing the lowly,'" of seeing itself in service to lesser dependents. Rome understood its benefactions as providing "communications, law and peace" and itself as the recipient of the world's gratitude and appreciation.[48] O'Donovan's stunning commentary on Augustine's analysis of pride reveals a complexity that far exceeds notions like will to power or even the desire to oppress. Rome's lust for admiration and ascendancy; its hunger for glory as the world's benefactor and therefore as the center of the world's gratitude and appreciation; its self-designation as the servant of the lowly; its willing acceptance of captivities brought on by demonic illusions; and the appetite for empire with its natural corollary of bondage to the sensual—all of these provide insight into pride not reducible to the will to power, and not even reducible to the lust for domination. Sin, indeed, is a complex weave and the strands of pride a polyester fabric of manifold threads.

47. Ibid., 79.
48. Ibid., 80.

Human Nature

In addition to Augustine's analysis of Rome, O'Donovan also draws on the New Testament to display protological accounts of sin, such as "sin as lawlessness"(1 John 3:4). But even more prevalent are "the various manifestations of sin in a broad phenomenal sweep, often in an eschatological framework (2 Tim 3:1ff.) In such passages O'Donovan points to "the collapse of sociality" as the breakdown of the organic character of the community where people become lovers of themselves to the exclusion of others. In these contexts, individualism does not precede social development, but rather follows it. Individualism represents a pulling back from communications, an act that begins in being consumed with material acquisitiveness, moving then to "aggressive competitiveness" and resulting in the breakdown of "relations of responsibility and trust, personal degradation, and godlessness."[49] With these comments O'Donovan further complicates the account of sin with its lawlessness, its broad sweep in a larger eschatological construct, its breakdown of the organic character of society, and its subsequent individualism expressed in withdrawing from communications, burning with a material acquisitiveness and aggressive competitiveness, dissolving commitments of responsibility and trust, and spinning into personal corruption and godlessness. This is a far more complex account of sin than that offered by Niebuhr's dualism of arrogance and sloth.

O'Donovan concludes that "a complete phenomenology of sin" requires more than "a single protological concept such as 'pride.'" He suggests that "the function of a protology is to *locate* sin in relation to the freedom of human agents vis-à-vis God, rather than to *describe* it." O'Donovan certainly understands that pride can be viewed as "the primal sin worked out in the will-to-power," that is, that such a dynamic occurs; he nevertheless maintains that attention to power alone is not adequate to the enormous complexity of pride and sin. Wielders of power can, indeed, be vitiated by pride, but they can also be contaminated by weakness, "indolence, compassion, or stupidity, by not having to take responsibility and by being protected from it by others."[50] O'Donovan also considers other dimensions of sin, including an appreciative view of Niebuhr's work on "the *collective* seat of the will-to-power" and also of other forms of sin in anarchy, loss of social discipline, narcissism, self-absorption, and so on.[51] My point here

---

49. Ibid.

50. Ibid., 80–81. O'Donovan's italics.

51. Ibid., 81–83. Parenthetically, I have problems with O'Donovan's notion of "the collective seat of the will to power." It is a high abstraction of its own and requires much more attention to the discourse and practices of the dynamics of power.

is that Niebuhr's understanding of the sin of overreaching transcendence, as pride, is too simple. Even when complemented by the sin of sensuality, Niebuhr's conception of sin still does not address this more "complex weave" O'Donovan identifies. Niebuhr's social theory not only proffers an inadequate conception of the self as constituting itself, but also (in part as a result of this view) an example of a too abstract and too simple approach to understanding sin. I am convinced that a radically more nuanced look must be given to the dynamics of the self than what Niebuhr offers. His view represents but a single, albeit complex, practice of introspection that, when taken as the singular representation of the human condition, ignores a far greater range of such practices. I turn now to this matter.

THE SELF-CONSCIOUS SELF

Let me begin with his notion of transcendence, which carries with it a highly self-focused, and often egoistic, self-consciousness in Niebuhr's thought. This is a highly reflective self, one given, I daresay, to intensive introspection, at least in the sense of making an object of itself and paying attention to its interests, its passions, and its impulses, not to mention the focus on its limitations in the pursuit or realization of all of these. The very freedom of the self in Niebuhr depends upon this self-conscious, introspective capacity to see itself in its settings, relationships, and circumstances. In fact, as we have seen, Niebuhr at one point makes the claim that *"man is a spirit who stands outside of nature, life, himself, his reason and the world."*[52] That is an extraordinary claim!

But my first question is whether Niebuhr's concept universally characterizes the self in all times and places. Not unlike Mahmood, anthropologist Talal Asad, for one, calls the legitimacy of universal characterizations of the self into question. Asad argues that "'agency' is a complex term whose senses emerge within semantic and institutional networks that define and make possible *particular* ways of relating to people, things, and one's self." In a discussion on resistance and empowerment he contends that cultural theory tends to make use of the idea of agency as a "metaphysical" concept of a conscious agent-subject who has both the ability and "the desire to go in a singular historical direction: that of increasing self-empowerment and decreasing pain."[53] (Asad uses the word *metaphysical* to mean, I take

52. *ND*1, 3. Italics mine.
53. *FS*, 79. See 67–79 for full discussion.

it, what one regards as "real.") Asad also observes that the concept of "interest," including "self-interest," is often treated as if it refers to something "universal, natural, essential." He cautions that the use of such categories requires careful reflection and qualification of them in different social circumstances.[54] In other words, Asad's contention is that these concepts are not universals, and for this reason he argues that it is necessary to take into account "how, by whom, and in what context the concept of agency is defined and used."[55] I shall turn to the issue of interest and self-interest later, but for now I simply want to register this significant point.

Key to Asad's view is his understanding of habitus, which he derives from Marcel Mauss. Habitus refers to "an embodied capacity that is more than physical ability" and "also includes cultivated sensibilities and passions, an orchestration of the senses." In other words, our dispositions, our sensibilities, the specific makeup of our passions, the composition and harmonization of our senses are embodied in us through the formation of a habitus. Further, habitus is to be thought of as "the passionate performance of an embodied ethical sensibility." It is not something we *choose* to adopt or not; rather, as Asad sees it, it is a dimension of what we "essentially" are and "must do." What needs to be understood here on Asad's point of view is that the habitus is not something the subject chooses or volitionally takes on. The habitus is intrinsic to the very construction of the subject; it is something the subject *is*. It is not a socialization of some "preexistent" or "existential" self; it is constitutive *of* the subject.[56]

Asad makes his claims about habitus in a context in which he is demonstrating the ways that the concepts of "the religious" and "the secular" are constructed and reconstructed, especially in relationship to pain and suffering. The shifts in these concepts and their relationship to other ideas such as responsibility and consciousness are necessary in reconsiderations of the meaning of these terms. This process, however, must not be "an abstract inquiry" into nothing more than alterations in language use, but an attempt to address questions about *how the body lives a range of human concerns* like "pain and punishment, compassion and pleasure, hope and fear."[57] I would add to this list how one lives a certain self-reflexivity and its sensibilities of limitation.

54. Ibid., 71 n. 9.
55. Ibid., 78–79.
56. Ibid., 95–96.
57. Ibid., 99. Italics mine.

Asad's discussion of habitus relates directly to Niebuhr's notion of the self as a composite of self-transcendent freedom and nature or finitude. Asad calls into question conceptions of the self that make self-consciousness the very essence of the self, as in the case of Niebuhr at least in terms of the freedom of the self. If nothing else, Asad sees such conceptions as too simple, too abstract, too uninhabited by the range of concepts, practices, linguistic usages, etc., that constitute consciousness itself. Moreover, for Asad freedom has much more to do with the capaciousness of an agent to work *with and in* the concepts, practices, and skills of a form of life than it does with a self-conscious subjectivity making choices among a range of options made into an object by the self.

I understand, to be clear, that in Niebuhr the self is not *only* spirit or transcendence, but is also nature and finitude. Niebuhr does not ignore the body in his understanding of the self. Yet for my present purposes, the important question is, *which* body is it? *Which* nature is it? Both nature and the body are highly mediated notions. And, in Niebuhr's arguments about finitude, *which* finitude is the focus of his work? I am suggesting here that there is a very specific conceptuality at work in both his views of transcendence or spirit and nature or finitude. Further, which complex grammar of concepts are finitude and self-reflexivity enmeshed within, and what is their relation? It is these concepts that require attention, especially with the practices in which they are embedded. Contra Niebuhr's claim, I am arguing that these are not universals in depicting the nature of the self, but rather they are concepts in Niebuhr's thought that have moved high up the ladder of abstraction. At this high level of abstraction these concepts generalize and, by that fact, obscure—when they do not excise—a great range of practices that can be gathered under labels like these.

PRACTICES OF INTROSPECTION

I contend that Niebuhr's understanding of the dynamics of the self needs to be seen as a *particular* practice of introspection rather than as representative of a (the) universal human condition or nature. What Niebuhr elaborates is not *the* practice of reflexivity, but a very specific set of practices of reflexivity bound by culture, time, and the social. Let us look at a few examples from an enormous range of practices of introspection that do not resemble those Niebuhr considered. Niebuhr tends to work with practices of introspection that focus on finitude in ways that generate anxiety. In contrast, a highly skilled, experienced craftsperson who works with wood does not, I daresay, see the limits of, say, what can be done with redwood in contrast to oak as an occasion of anxiety. Rather, the limitations the craftsperson faces in working with different kinds of wood are occasions for the display of skill. This capacity to reflect on the various limits and possibilities of oak and redwood and of his or her capacities to work with them are not caught in any coherent way in the tensions of transcendence and finitude that Niebuhr depicts. To the contrary, reflecting on these limitations leads the craftsperson to realize the opportunities to be creative with the differences each of these materials offers. The differences in types of wood can in fact be an occasion of delight for a skilled woodworker. Anxiety does not necessarily enter this situation.

I am aware, of course, that Niebuhr sees the dynamics of transcendence and finitude as a source of creativity as well as destruction. My point here, however, is to draw from the example of a skilled woodworker to suggest a range of practices of self-reflexivity and an active appreciation for a host of limitations. I cannot help thinking about how different the conceptuality and the practices are when one moves from a woodworker, to a carpenter, to an electrician, to a plumber, to a bricklayer, to a cook, to a hairdresser, to a parent, and so forth. The range of concepts, the radical difference in the practices indicated in them, the character of reflexivity, and the ranges of limitations that accompany each are enormous. But, even more, I think of practices of touch, of skill, of sizing up a situation, of forms of reasoning about a practice, and of an implicit knowing, meaning a grasp of circumstances that cannot be put in representative language: these are but a few of the practices that do not necessarily involve self-reflexivity in making an object of the self, but a habitus of work that is more often "automatic."

Another illustration, one I have chosen from two of Niebuhr's contemporaries: Richard Sennett and Jonathan Cobb, in their book *The Hidden Injuries of Class*, report on a dynamic of working people, the jobs they do, and their attitudes about them. Specifically, Sennett and Cobb focus on those institutional settings where a worker's freedom of action is limited in ways that threaten him or her with reprimand or, perhaps, loss of employment. As a result, these workers construct two spheres of being within themselves on the job. The one is what they do in direct relationship to their bosses in the workplace; in this sphere they do not talk about what "I did" when discussing the completion of a given piece of work that they did in fact do, but rather talk about this situation "being straightened out." This more passive way of talking replaces the "I." In contrast, the use of "I" is reserved for places where the worker would be "the master of the situation."[58] In this construction of two spheres by the self, the worker is able to separate "the real person from the institution's individual" and hence to prevent becoming an "institutional man."[59] Now, this certainly is a practice of introspection, but it does not match Niebuhr's view of human nature in which the tension between transcendence and finitude results in an anxiety where the worker escapes into arrogance or sloth.

I realize that a Niebuhrian could interpret this situation as one in which the workers' use of passive language and the refusal to use "I" language could be read as sloth. It certainly can sound like passivity, and perhaps in some situations it is. But in the treatment given it by Sennett and Cobb, it sounds much more like coping and survival on the job and the protection of self-respect and dignity. To reinterpret this in Niebuhr's categories—in effect, to tell these workers what they *really* are doing—is an imperialistic hermeneutics.

Another example: Mahmood examines the relationship between emulation and reflexivity among mosque movement women. She observes that critics often put down these women because they see the women as substituting the emulation of certain "exemplary standards" instead of operating from what they "really feel." For instance, they are criticized for a ritual of weeping because their "sincerity of intent" is called into question, with this ritualized behavior being interpreted by their critics as acts of pretension. Mahmood, however, counters that these acts "were not only expressions of their interiorized religiosity but also a necessary means of acquiring it." The repeated, ritualized behavioral acts of weeping furnish the self: these "bodily acts" are not understood primarily as an indication of what they feel inside, but rather they are a way to acquire a "potentiality," a capacity, which is gained by means of certain types of training and knowledge.[60]

Furthermore, some Muslim women criticize the mosque movement women because they believe that a ritual of weeping ought not to be thoughtlessly reproduced, but rather ought to be an occasion upon which one might reflect upon one's "true I." The concept with which these critics operate is one in which the self in its essential makeup is to be realized or

---

58. *Hidden Injuries of Class*, 193.

59. Ibid., 197.

60. *PP*, 146–47.

Human Nature

fulfilled. The mosque movement women, however, understood such ritual behavior as an opportunity to "transcend the 'I,'" that is, the "I" caught up "in ephemeral pleasures and pursuits." Mahmood concludes that self-reflection in this ritual behavior seeks to mold the "I" in accord with the authoritative claims of Islam and to do so through practices intrinsic to Muslim tradition so that these women embody their faith: "In other words, bodily form in this view does not simply represent the interiority (as it does for [some critics of these women]), but serves as the 'developable' means... through which certain kinds of ethical and moral capacities are attained."[61]

I take from Mahmood's discussion that reflexivity is a highly complex practice that varies not only across but within cultures. The introspection of women who wish to emulate exemplary people of their religious tradition, who wish to form themselves in capacious, embodied sensitivities, sensibilities, and behavioral acts simply cannot be equated with Niebuhr's universal, existential self. I realize, again, that a Niebuhrian may rush to point to the sloth and arrogance operative in such a movement as that of the mosque women, but these women have concepts and teaching to address issues of pride and passivity and hence do not need a structured self as alien as that of Niebuhr. To persistently impose Niebuhr's rendering of the self as a composite of nature and spirit seems to have a "taint" of colonial interpretation.

One last example will have to suffice. The kind of introspection that Niebuhr describes requires a self-conscious, analytic form of introspection. It involves a form of reflective practice that is not pervasive in human introspection and requires a degree of inner exploration not characteristic of all societies or cultures. For example, Walter Ong, in his classic text *The Presence of the Word*, discusses the ways in which "human concepts" adapt to the "psychological structures of the milieu" wherein they form. Ong works with the concept of the "sensorium," which he uses to refer to the cultural and historical organization of the senses. He reports that when the sensorium changes in different historical epochs, concepts change accordingly.[62]

His focus here and in his later *Orality and Literacy* is on the differences between oral, literate, and electronic cultures. In this subsequent book, in a discussion of the "person-interactive" context of oral culture, Ong observes that "primary orality fosters personality structures that in certain ways are more communal and externalized, and *less introspective*

61. Ibid., 147–48. Her reference to Asad here is his *Geneaologies of Religion*.
62. *Presence of the Word*, 190.

than those common among literates."[63] He points out that communication in oral cultures "unites people and groups," while in literate cultures writing and reading are "solitary activities" that throw the psyche back on itself. In an interesting example he reports differences in schizophrenia between oral and literate cultures. In the former schizoid behavior tends to be externalized, whereas in the latter it is interiorized. Schizophrenic literates tend toward "psychic withdrawal into a dream world of their own" (hence loss of contact with their surroundings), whereas people in an oral culture display rather "extreme external confusion," which is manifested in overt acts of violence, such as mutilation of oneself and of other people.[64]

My point here is not that people in oral cultures never engage in introspection or think in a calculated way about their own advantages. Marcel Mauss explores potlatch ceremonies in various cultures, and he argues that these rituals of wealth destruction are certainly not characterized by "complete detachment." They are not, as he says, "without egoism."[65] My point, rather, is that these practices of introspection cannot be reduced to the tension of transcendence and finitude on the Niebuhrian model. What is required instead is close attention to the practices of introspection at work, the grammar of concepts in use, and the form of life in which these occur.

THE REGISTERS OF SUBJECTIVITY

Finally, I turn to the work of William E. Connolly and his analysis of the formation of the subject, especially in political life. Connolly examines subjectivity and intersubjectivity in terms of several "registers of appraisal" that operate in political engagement. Convinced that the discourse of politics cannot be reduced simply to rational means of deliberation, his aim is to delineate "the layered intricacy of thinking and judgment," looking at both the positive and the negative roles these can play and examining what he calls "the visceral register of subjectivity." This gut level of subjectivity is complex. It certainly involves feelings, but it also involves "intensities." These intensities are characterized by urgency and fervency but may not be expressible in representative language. Connolly calls these "pre-representational sites of appraisal" a "secondary register of intersubjectivity."[66] Thus

63. *Orality and Literacy*, 69. Italics mine.
64. Ibid.
65. *Gift*, 74.
66. *WIANS*, 26.

there are "thought-imbued feelings," but there are also "thought imbued intensities, below the reach of feeling." He distinguishes here the sensible from the infrasensible, with the former existing at the level of appearance and capable of being described in representative language, and the latter operating below the level of appearance, not usually available to representative language, and "only partly and precariously susceptible to direct overview and control." Nevertheless, this visceral register at the level of the infrasensible has "significant effects" on "thought, images, feelings, desires, passions, and concepts."[67] While these visceral modes of appraisal cannot always be put in language—that is, representative language—they can be powerfully efficacious.

Connolly uses here the illustration of disgust. He observes that "we think with our stomachs," and, using contemporary brain research, he reports that the stomach is connected to "a simple cortical organization of its own." He states, "This infrasensible center stores thought-imbued feelings of sadness, anxiety, happiness, disgust, anger, and revenge to be activated under particular circumstances"—as when, for example, an intense feeling of disgust rises up when you observe someone picking his nose and eating the contents.[68]

Research by neurophysiologist Joseph LeDoux on a small brain just beneath the cortex, the amygdala, and its relationship to the prefrontal cortex, the "large brain" that is highly developed in humans, discovered that each of these take signals from the same places in the body, but they respond to them differently. The amygdala reacts immediately, but rather crudely and with potent energy. A signal similar to some terrifying moment or frantic event will "pass like greased lightning over the potentiated pathways to the amygdala, unleashing the fear reaction."[69] The prefrontal cortex, however, responds more slowly and puts the signal through "a sophisticated linguistic network in a more refined way and forming a more complex judgment. The amygdala also projects its response to the signal and a good deal of its intensity to the prefrontal cortex." But, says LeDoux, "the amygdala has a greater influence on the cortex than the cortex has on the amygdala, allowing emotional arousal to dominate and control thinking. . . . Although thoughts can easily trigger emotions (by activating the

---

67. Ibid., 175.
68. Ibid.
69. *Emotional Brain*, 258. Quoted in Connolly, *WIANS*, 28.

amygdala), we are not very effective at willfully turning off emotions (by deactivating the amygdala).["]70

My point here is not that we should substitute LeDoux's research for Niebuhr's point of view. The brain research of today quickly becomes superseded tomorrow. What can be said is that neuroscience opens a new door for reflection on the self, the subject, and agency. It cannot be ignored. As such, it adds a new range of issues to be addressed not only personally, but intersubjectively and, as Connolly has so powerfully described, politically. These registers of subjectivity and intersubjectivity bring before us a great range of questions and dynamics that open up the field of politics, for example, in many new ways. It is not therefore that we simply snatch up brain research and substitute it for a theological or social understanding of the self or sin, but rather that it offers new opportunities to reflect on "the complex weave" of sin and the layers and complexities of subjectivity and intersubjectivity in directions Niebuhr does not offer.

CONCLUSION

In conclusion, I challenge Niebuhr's view of human nature, with its understanding of the self as a composite of spirit and nature characterized by the dynamics of a dialectic between transcendence and finitude that results in anxiety and tempts the self to escape from the one into arrogance and the other into sensuality. He understands the self as constituting, as individuated, as existentially "prior," one that is the primary source of human evil in the world because these existential dynamics are compounded in group life and are constant in their fundamental character throughout human cultures and history.

I offer an alternative view, not the self of Niebuhr, but a subject constituted in the discourses and practices of a form of life. This subject is not a constituting self displaying the dynamics of its nature in every time and place, but a constituted subject that takes on agency in the "semantic and institutional networks that define and make possible particular ways of relating to people, things, and one's self."[71] This subject-agent cannot be reduced to the binary structure of Niebuhr's existential self, but rather emerges with a far more complex weave in the "phenomenology of sin," where various practices of reflexivity are at work, where limitations are quite widely con-

70. Ibid., 303. Quoted in Connolly, *WIANS*, 29.
71. Asad, *FS*, 78.

ceived, where the practices of introspection can vary indeterminately in human terms, and where layers of subjectivity and intersubjectivity greatly complicate essential views of the self built on binary oppositions.

With the kind of self I have described in view, where then does this leave us with a matter like self-interest, which figures so prominently in Niebuhr's analysis? How, indeed, can one challenge the role that self-interest plays in personal and social life? What is the status of self-interest with the view of the subject-agent I suggest thus far? Surely Niebuhrian realism brings a bracing sophistication, a searing, self-evident empiricism to any examination of the human condition with all its ambition, greed, and self-seeking. I turn next to an examination of Niebuhr's understanding of interest and to a critical examination of his views on this crucial issue.

2

Niebuhr's View of Interest

COMMENTS ON NIEBUHR'S "METHOD" raise interesting questions about his definitions and uses of concepts. Robin Lovin, for example, states that Niebuhr "gives little time to definitions,"[1] and Larry Rasmussen says, "Theological method and careful definition of categories evidently belong to 'the fine points of pure theology,'" to which Niebuhr gives little attention.[2] Ronald Stone speaks of Niebuhr's "equivocal usage" of key terms such as "national interests, power, imperialism, liberalism, conservatism, idealism, and realism," and of Niebuhr's hesitation "to define rigorously and to adhere to the definitions."[3]

In terms of Niebuhr's more general approach of "dialectical thought," Niebuhr believes, says William John Wolf, that the more profound "truths about man [sic], history, and reality" must be expressed so as to address adequately "contradictory or seemingly contradictory aspects of reality."[4] Other critics, however—and very prominent ones at that—are less theoretical. Paul Tillich, for example, says, "Reinie never tells us how he knows; he

---

1. *RNCR*, 3.
2. *RNTPL*, 17.
3. *RNPP*, 215. Cf. 180.
4. William John Wolf, "Reinhold Niebuhr's Doctrine of Man," in Kegley and Bretall, *RN*, 231. But Wolf describes Niebuhr's thought as "relational" rather than dialectical, suggesting that "a somewhat stylized Niebuhrian analysis is to state two opposite facets of the problem, then to reduce each further to negative and positive elements, to correlate the subjugation of the basic affirmation with the sub-positive of the basic negation, then to show how the Christian answer meets these complexities, but only in the wholeness of the problem; for once any one element of the Christian answer is emphasized at the expense of some other facet, distortion occurs." *RN*, 231.

just starts knowing."⁵ H. Richard Niebuhr explains that the problem of "understanding" his brother grows from the fact that his presuppositions are concealed "like a great iceberg of which three-fourths or more is beneath the surface and in which what's expressly said depends on something that is not made explicit."⁶

In *Reinhold Niebuhr and Christian Realism* Lovin describes Niebuhr's aims in his work as "synthetic" in the sense of connecting "related ideas into a complex whole, rather than strictly delimiting the individual elements." In this way the clarification of concepts occurs through the process of naming what they exclude, and the elucidation of a position by what it specifically rejects. Lovin indicates that Niebuhr's synthetic methodology is especially apparent in the way he uses the term *Christian Realism*. Lovin's basic argument is that Niebuhr's point of view is comprised of political realism, moral realism, and theological (really Christian) realism and that these three elements are "mutually reinforcing, rather than systematically related" in his thought.⁷

NIEBUHR'S USES OF INTEREST

Nowhere are these methodological observations more apparent than in the way that Niebuhr deals with the concept of interest. In this chapter I name key aspects of Niebuhr's understanding of interest, yet I am not aware of any place in his writing where he actually defines the term as such.

Let me be clear, it is not my wish that Niebuhr give us some universal definition of interest that will capture its essential meaning. I do not believe that such a definition can be developed. What I do wish for is more clarity about how the concept is used by Niebuhr and greater clarity about connections he makes between these different uses.

Many times I find myself wishing for more connections between various types of interests in his thought, or for some more descriptive way of addressing the complexities of his view of this central concept. Indeed, when I read Niebuhr I often feel that I am in a dark night, and his comments are like lightning bolts that illuminate the landscape. As indebted as I am for such explosions of light, I discover, come morning, that while I recognize the same countryside, it nevertheless looks different or, at least,

---

5. Quoted in Rasmussen, *RNTPL*, 17.
6. Quoted in Stone, *RNPP*, 132.
7. *RNCR*, 3–4.

more complicated. This has been my experience with his uses of the word *interest*. There can be no doubt that a great strength of Niebuhr's mind is his brilliant insight—a brilliance that was often displayed along with an equally remarkable capacity for stunning generalization. As with many people, one's greatest strength can be the location of one's greatest weakness. For this reason, to grasp fully how Niebuhr understands and what he means by the term *interest* (sometimes also rendered *self-interest*), we will need to examine how he uses *interest* in a wide range of contexts. In the following pages I will treat ten different ways that he uses this concept. I do not claim that my treatment is fully exhaustive of every way Niebuhr ever used the concept, but I believe that identifying these ten ways establishes the enormous elasticity of the concept in Niebuhr's corpus.

1. Resistance to Established Norms

Lovin calls attention to a quote from Niebuhr where, as he says, Niebuhr's "dialectical method yields almost definitional specificity"—a "rare point," Lovin admits. This moment of specificity occurs in Niebuhr's essay titled "Augustine's Political Realism," in which he discusses the distinction between political and metaphysical realism. Niebuhr writes:

> In political and moral theory "realism" denotes the disposition to take all factors in a social and political situation, which offer resistance to established norms, into account, particularly the factors of self-interest and power. . . ."Idealism" is, in the esteem of its proponents, characterized by loyalty to moral norms and ideals, rather than to self-interest, whether individual or collective. It is, in the opinion of its critics, characterized by the disposition to ignore or be indifferent to the forces in human life which offer resistance to universally valid ideals and norms.[8]

I find Lovin's characterization of this passage to be quite apt. It is remarkably clear, at least for Niebuhr; it is *almost* a definition, but not quite. Having gone through Niebuhr's books and no few articles looking for a careful definition of the term *interest*, I have not found anything better than this quote to which Lovin calls attention. My conclusion is that the best approach is to look at the nomenclature Niebuhr employs for the concept of

---

8. Niebuhr, "Augustine's Political Realism," 119–20. Quoted in Lovin, *RNCR*, 3–4. Italics mine. This essay appears in Niebuhr's *Christian Realism and Political Problems*, 119–46.

interest and to attempt some understanding of his notion of interest by his usage of such terminology. In this particular almost-but-not-quite definition of realism, one gathers that interest is one of the two important factors (the other being power, which I treat in chapters 3, 4, and 5) that resists "universally valid ideals and norms."

2. Classifications of Interests

The word *interest* occurs often in Niebuhr's work. Readers might expect, given his dialectical thought, that the word would typically occur in opposition to some other concept, like norms, ideals, moral commitments, religious claims, etc. This frequently is the case, yet what is perhaps more interesting is the fact that Niebuhr typically uses the concept of interest by making sharp—sometimes dialectic—distinctions within the concept itself, or by elaborating its various dimensions. I think here of individual/group interests, of specific/general interest, of lower/higher interests, of self/larger interests, of self/general interests, of local/national interests, of creative or constructive interests/selfish interests, of conflicting interests/coincidence of interests, of false/real interests, etc. It is clear from these classifications within the concept of interest that Niebuhr has a very complex understanding of interest—that is, he is not working with a flat conception of what interest is or how it is used.

What is not so clear, however, is how his use of the concept—when writing of interest as higher, larger, creative, etc.—necessarily entails resistance to established norms. In fact, a good case can be made for interests classified in these ways to be often *in concert with* established norms rather than posing resistance to them. It would seem, then, that interests that are resistant to established norms would more likely be those that were self-interests—that is, narrow interests, individual interests, specific interests, and, in an international context, national interests. Yet, I daresay that one can also make the case that selfish, narrow interests can be integrated into an established status quo and integrated with certain kinds of established norms. It seems to me quite clear that narrow interests in the sense of privileging advantages for certain groups are often built into an established status quo.

3. Self-Regard

Surely, however, when Niebuhr speaks of interests as resistant to morality, ideals, established norms, and so on, he is referring to the power of self-regard working itself out through interests. In his *Faith and History* he refers repeatedly to the power of self-regard and describes it as "the root of sin (excessive concern for the self)."[9] This assessment of self-regard grows out of Niebuhr's understanding of human nature. He acknowledges that the transcendence of the self provides a certain kind of release from natural necessities so that individuals are not absolutely bound to follow natural impulses or self-interest; nevertheless, he also maintains that "the self seeks its own despite its freedom to envisage a wider good than its own interest." The freedom by which one could transcend self-seeking continues to be used in such a way as to expand the fulfillment of the self's own interests.

This dynamic Niebuhr identifies as egoism. In his view, such human egoism is not a function of nature. Rather the dynamics of the self are such that "nature's survival impulse" can be changed into a far more powerful, devastating, devious, and wide-ranging impulse of self-seeking than the more "one-dimensional survival impulse of nature."[10] In other words, human egoism grows out of the existential dynamics of the self, and these dynamics can feed on the more natural survival impulse. The very freedom of the self includes a tendency of the self to make itself the "false center of existence"—a tendency that Niebuhr identifies as "a corruption of self-concern."[11] This tendency is, as Niebuhr famously asserts, compounded in human group life. This is the inclination "of every collective, whether tribe, nation, or empire, to make itself the center of universal history."[12] It should not be surprising, then, that for Niebuhr this self-regard is bound up with idolatry, that is, self-worship,[13] or, in other words, in an excessive regard for self that thereby attempts "to usurp the prerogatives of God."[14] Indeed, when the self takes on such pretensions, it is tantamount to the self presuming divine prerogatives, and in so presuming it becomes the most dangerous form of arrogance.[15]

9. *FH*, 176.
10. Ibid., 93–95.
11. *SDH*, 255.
12. *FH*, 113.
13. Ibid., 125.
14. Ibid., 121.
15. Ibid., 173.

Niebuhr contends that this inclination to make self and one's collective group the center of existence, with all of its propensities to idolatry, is a major source of illusion, especially among those who seem to believe that these pervasive and ongoing factors of self- and parochial interest either have been overcome or can be eliminated. Niebuhr states that in the American culture of his time the problem is with those who believe that human self-regard can be reduced to "the force of immediate human needs." According to Niebuhr, such views focus on "the perennial necessities of survival, the hungers and thirst of man [sic]" even as they fail to distinguish "the economic motive" from "the power impulse." While claims that self- and parochial interests can be overcome and eliminated and may recognize human beings even as "a beast of prey," Niebuhr insists that such claims fail to recognize the self "as a creature of time who is troubled with visions of the absolute and is torn by contradictory impulses between subjecting his finite life to someone or something greater than himself, and claiming the possession of some unconditional ground of virtue and wisdom from which he can survey his fellow men [sic] and hold them in contempt." Modern culture simply does not conceive how intimately related these impulses of the self are and with them how inextricably related human creativity and destructiveness really are.[16]

Basic to Niebuhr's point here is that it is always the *entire* person "who is engaged in such creativity and destruction."[17] Neither an impulse, nor a need, nor some isolated drive, nor some historically or culturally limited propensity can account for the human predicament. This predicament, this creativity and destruction, reside, rather, in the very nature of the human being, in the dynamics of the human self capable of self-consciousness and of a certain transcendence over itself and its world; but it is this self that is nonetheless haunted by anxiety about its finitude and death and is ever searching for escape, either through all the subtle forms of a self-elevated arrogance or through the self-loss and passivity of the impulses and compulsions of sensuality.

4. The Rational Calculation of Advantage/Gain

This focus on self-regard in Niebuhr seems to involve an implicit preoccupation of the self with its own rational calculation of advantage and gain,

16. *SDH*, 173–74.
17. Ibid., 174.

but also in some cases of a more explicit statement of these calculations. For example, Niebuhr writes of "the inclination of men [sic] to take advantage of each other."[18] Yet he also argues that the notion of justice presupposes a tendency for the concerns of some members of a community to be more engaged "with their own weal than with that of others." He states that such limitations are required in more "complex relations" where two—a remarkably low threshold—or more persons are involved. Consequently, as a result of this tendency, "all systems of justice make careful distinctions between the rights and interests of various members of the community." The function of these distinctions is to limit the capacity of humans to take advantage of each other, which Niebuhr sees as "the symbols of the spirit of justice." At the same time, even when harmony is achieved through such limitations, the resultant justice is only, according to Niebuhr, "an approximation of brotherhood." Nonetheless, such an approximation remains "the best possible harmony" given the predicaments that result from a pervasive "human egoism."[19]

Thus, while rational calculation of advantages is necessary to creating the conditions for "a tolerable justice," agape, or sacrificial love, stands ever in contradiction to "the natural and justified inclination of the self to preserve and defend its own existence." Niebuhr argues that agape ever confuses "the nicely calculated balances and discrimination of competing interests" of such a necessary but always relative justice.[20] Niebuhr also argues in a discussion of sacrificial love that "mutual love and loyalty" constitute "the highest possibilities of social life," insofar as they transcend "the rational calculations and the power balances of a rough justice." Indeed, mutual love requires constant nourishment by "impulses of grace," without which the "calculation of mutual advantages" and their "mutual relations" devolve into nothing more than "true calculation of such advantages," and then into a consequent resentment since no "complete reciprocity in all actual relations" is possible.[21]

It is important, finally, to note at least two significant limitations to the role of the rational calculation of interest in Niebuhr's thought. First, such calculations of interests do not stand alone, but rather are a part of what he calls the "equilibrium of social forces," a concept that includes the

18. *FH*, 189.
19. *NDM2*, 251–52.
20. *FH*, 174.
21. Ibid., 185.

power arrangements, the vitalities of human life, and the threat and use of force. Niebuhr asserts, "The rational calculation of the powers and vitalities involved in a social situation is thus an inevitable accompaniment of the rational calculation of rights and interests involved in a socio-moral problem."[22] As pervasive as interests are in individual and social life, they are not the only factor in Niebuhr's thought.

A second limitation resides in what Niebuhr characterizes as "the contingent and finite character of rational estimates of rights and interests." Here Niebuhr acknowledges some limitation in the capacity of human rationality itself to assess not only rightful claims, but advantage and gain.[23] Early in his career, in *Moral Man and Immoral Society*, Niebuhr maintains that "reason is always, to some degree, the servant of the self in a social situation," yet even that servitude of reason and its master, the self, cannot escape the finitude of all things human and, for that matter, all of creation.[24] Later, in *The Nature and Destiny of Man*, Niebuhr makes this same point when he claims that "there is no universal reason in history and no impartial perspective upon the whole field of vital interests, which compete with and mutually support each other."[25] Apparently, our limitations in rationally assessing the interest of others apply as well to our capacity to assess rationally our own advantages and gain, although, to be sure, the motivation, on Niebuhr's understanding, is much more pervasive and stronger for the latter than the former.

5. Self-Interest and Common Grace

Another key use in Niebuhr's understanding of self-interest is its relationship to common grace. In this connection, Niebuhr holds to a reality of "common grace" that prevents a "consistent self-destruction through self-seeking," which, without such grace, would otherwise characterize ordinary life. Included in this concept are "family and communal responsibilities, affections, disciplines and pressures." These are related to agape "as the ultimate norm," but more specifically they play a creative role in connecting life to life and contribute to "the health of the self" by drawing it into relationships and commitments larger than the discrete, self-contained

22. *NDM2*, 259–60.
23. Ibid., 252.
24. *MMIS*, xiv–xv.
25. *NDM2*, 252.

individual. Yet Niebuhr immediately cautions that such relationships and commitments nevertheless also remain "fruitful sources of collective egotism, being used by the self to make inordinate collective claims after disavowing individual ones."[26] Relationships are thus essential to how the self achieves transcendence and genuine connection with others, even as such transcendence and connection are by no means a panacea for human tendencies towards egoism and injustice.

Late in his life Niebuhr continues to hold that while the law of love remains the foundation of moral life, obedience to it "by a simple act of will" does not occur for the reason that "the power of self-concern" is too strong. What he calls "the forces of common grace" mediate the power of self-concern, pulling the self "from its undue self-concern." Niebuhr's appreciation for common grace leads him to believe that the Christian concept of saving grace has been too sharply distinguished from a more common and not distinctly religious or Christian concept of grace, and overemphasized in these supposed differences.[27]

6. The Distorting Impact of Interests

Basic to Niebuhr's use of interest is the distortive effect it has on individual and social life. He names a number of factors that contribute to how this distortion that attends interest occurs—namely, pride and pretension, personal deception and the deceit of others, overestimation of the self's virtue, conscious and unconscious factors, self-worship, delusion and illusion, and the fragmentary, ambiguous, and contingent character of life and history. Lovin observes that often the most prominent feature of Niebuhr's political analysis is his sustained effort "to unmask distortions of justice caused by self-interest."[28] Let us examine a few examples.

One such distortion of justice that Niebuhr attributes to interest is the entrenched tendency of individuals to rationalize their interests and then, subsequently, to attempt to deceive others by such rationalization. For instance, Niebuhr argues that "all historic schemes of justice embody sinful elements" insofar as such schemes always include "implicit rationalizations of special interests."[29] Sometimes, this occurs because human beings "are

26. FH, 174–75.
27. MNHC, 125.
28. RNCR, 198.
29. FH, 193–94. Cf. NDM2, 252–56; MNHC, 30–83.

inclined to take the moral pretensions of themselves or their fellow man [*sic*] at face value." At other times, there is "the disposition to hide self-interest behind the façade of pretended devotion to values." According to Niebuhr, this disingenuous attempt to transcend self-interest is "well-nigh universal." Further, rationalization and its closely related ally, hypocrisy, represent two of the chief characteristics of the nation-state.[30]

Dishonesty, hypocrisy, and deceit have for Niebuhr, of course, a deeper source in the existential dynamics of the self, in its escape from anxiety through arrogance. In a discussion of the relation between dishonesty and pride Niebuhr claims that "while such deception is constantly directed against competing wills, seeking to secure their acceptance and validation of the self's generous opinion of itself, its primary purpose is to deceive, not others, but the self. The self must at any rate deceive itself first. Its deception of others is partly an effort to convince itself against itself."[31] Thus the distortions of self-interest begin with the self even as they "serve" the self in the subtleties of its arrogance and sensuality. Indeed, the capacity of interest to deceive is pervasive in the self and in its relations to others.

7. The Taint of Interest/Ideology

Phrases that occur in Niebuhr's work across the sweep of his mature writing include "the taint of interest," "the taint of ideology," and "the taint of passions."[32] As we will see below, Niebuhr believes that the principle of equality can function as a certain kind of limit on self-interest because of the way that, in his view, it stands at the height of the ideal of justice. As such, Niebuhr contends that the principle of equality "implicitly points towards love as the final form of justice; for equal justice is the approximation of brotherhood under the conditions of sin."[33] At the same time, he holds that the principle of equal justice can never be fully realized in history, because, in part, it suffers from an "inevitable 'ideological taint.'" For instance, one class will argue for the "absolute validity" of the principle of equal justice in the service of its interests, while another class will underscore the impossibility of its complete achievement—again, so as to serve its own

---

30. Niebuhr, in Brown, *ERN*, 123.

31. *NDM*1, 203. See the discussion in this important section, 203–7.

32. For example, *NDM*1, 182, *NDM*2, 252, 254–55; *SDH*, 214–16; Niebuhr, *ERN*, 132; *FH*, 186, 187; *MNHC*, 37, 51.

33. *NDM*2, 254.

interest. Such a circumstance, remarks Niebuhr, illustrates the operation of "ideological taint," even in the employment of a broadly appropriate principle, and even when that principle quite clearly transcends more narrow interests.[34]

In another context, Niebuhr demonstrates the way in which this "taint" is used to advantage by one group in its calculation—or, really, miscalculation—of the rights or interests of others.[35] He also speaks to "the taint of interest" when referring to the way that individuals and social groups conjure rationales that justify certain claims and translate "privileges into rights." In circumstances like these, what Niebuhr calls "a normal justice" is often, in fact, a *biased* framing of social circumstances on behalf of the gains of one particular party or group at the expense of another.[36] Niebuhr claims, moreover, that "the ideological taint of self-interest" is a universal phenomenon, occurring even "in the most rationally conceived social standards." Hence he believes that the pervasive close ties of self-love and reason—as seen in the taint of self-interest—provide a basis for supporting political realism in its advocacy against "most idealistic theories," and clearly with "all consistently idealistic theories."[37] Though it is not Niebuhr's position that human beings will always pursue their self-interests "in defiance of the community," he contends nonetheless that individuals do "interpret the interests of the community with a reason tainted by considerations of their own interests."[38]

8. The Limits of Self-Interest

The prevalence of self-interest notwithstanding, it would be a mistake to see self-interest as the single driving force of the individual and social life of human beings. For one thing, Niebuhr argues that humans have such a "strong . . . sense of obligation" to other human beings that they cannot seek their own interests without the pretension that they are doing so for the sake of others.[39] Toward the end of his life, he observes that "hypocrisy . . . is a tribute paid by the less acceptable impulse to the more acceptable

34. Ibid., 255.
35. Ibid., 252; cf. *FH*, 186.
36. *FH*, 187.
37. *MNHC*, 51.
38. *SDH*, 214–15.
39. Niebuhr, *ERN*, 123.

one." Further, Niebuhr concludes that the hypocrisy of both nations and individuals may point to "a residual creative capacity of their freedom." While this creative capacity is not "equal to" the impulse of self-regard, it is not "defaced" or destroyed by it either.[40]

In Niebuhr's work, the interests of one party can, of course, function in such a way as to impose real limits on the interest of another. But more important for my purposes is the relationship of wider or long-term interest to the narrower, short-term interests of a party. In a reflection on Augustine, Niebuhr characterizes this limiting function as "the leavening influence of a higher upon the lower loyalty or love," and claims that such leavening can prevent the "self-defeat" of a myopic realism that attends to its own interests, while failing to grasp the extent to which those interests are caught up in the interests of another party. Niebuhr is critical here of certain unnamed modern realists who, in reaction against "abstract and vague forms of international idealism," urge the nation-state to consider "only its own interests." Niebuhr acknowledges that calling the nation to its self-interest may seem unnecessary, yet he explains his conviction that "a consistent self-interest on the part of the nation will work against its interest because it will fail to do justice to the broader and longer-term interests, which are involved with the interests of other nations." Exclusive attention to narrow loyalties and interests by the nation conceal long-term interests, especially for those countries engaged with other free nations.[41] Thus Niebuhr considers many modern realists, while knowing "the power of collective self-interest," to be unable to comprehend the "blindness" of a position that does not conceive of self-interest in the multidimensional fashion that he favored.[42]

I will be remiss if I do not speak to the limitations of interest by the passions, vitalities, and norms. I must admit, however, that sorting out the passions, the vitalities, and interests is no simple matter. (I will come to the norms last.) In terms of the passions and vitalities, I do not find Niebuhr clear in his distinctions here, as I shall suggest in his discussion of sexuality below. Part of the problem, as we have seen, is that he does not provide carefully construed usages on the basis of which we can make such distinctions. Certainly with his understanding of the goodness of creation, natural impulses or instincts—I daresay even passions—are good and not evil in

---

40. *MNHS*, 75.
41. Niebuhr, *ERN*, 134.
42. Ibid., 140.

themselves. So "natural" vitalities and passions as such are not evil or sinful. At the same time, nature and spirit are a unity in human beings. Even when it comes to "natural" vitalities and passions, these are always infused with spirit, as indeed spirit is infused with nature, and hence "natural" vitalities and passions never appear in a pure, natural form in human beings.

One of his most illuminating discussions of vitalities and passions takes place in the context of his characterization of sexual passion in a discussion on sin as sensuality. He states that "the sexual, as every other physical, impulse in man [sic] is subject to and compounded with the freedom of man's [sic] spirit." The sexual impulse, he continues, is not reducible to simply the "glandular and physiological"; rather he maintains that, as with everything natural in humanity, the force of the sexual attains "the highest pinnacles of human spirituality." Be that as it may, human insecurity in the very capaciousness of freedom descends into the lowest reaches of human existence as "an instrument of compensation" and even as an escape from the self.[43] The point is that human sexuality is ever a mix of spirit and nature and of vitality and form, and of all of these ever engaged in the human existential predicament. It is important to note that Niebuhr does not say that sex is "as such" sinful. He understands primal sin as disobedience to God, and self-love as a basic expression of this disobedience. Hence, with "the harmony of nature" existentially "disturbed" by human self-love, Niebuhr maintains that sexual impulses become "particularly effective tools for both the assertion of the self and the flight from the self."[44] In conclusion Niebuhr states that "what sex reveals in regard to sensuality is not unique but typical in regard to the problem of sensuality in general"—namely, that sexuality is, first, the reach of self-love to such an extent that it "defeats its own ends"; second, an attempt "to escape the prison house of self" through finding an idol in some "process or person outside the self"; and third, an attempt to flee the confusion brought by sin "into some form of subconscious existence."[45] So while not sinful in itself, the sexual impulse does not existentially avoid sin in its expression.

Returning to the limits of interests, on the basis of Niebuhr's claims about the passions and the vitalities on the "natural" dimensions of humanity's synthesis of nature and spirit, we can now see that human interests can be fueled, indeed fired, by passions and vitalities. At the same time, it is

43. *NDM*1, 235f.
44. Ibid., 236–37.
45. Ibid., 239–40. Italics mine. See also, *MNHC*, 48; *SNE*, 132, 298.

also apparent that the dynamics of the sensuality of the self in its pursuit of self-defeating ends, in its devotion to idols, in its passivity and self-loss, and in its flights into subconscious existence can also readily, if not somewhat paradoxically, constitute powerful limitations on human interests as well. It is hardly news that the passions and vitalities not only distract and limit the interests of human beings but also can overwhelm, for example, the rational calculation of advantage and gain. To ignore these dynamics by focusing too centrally on interests, and to fail to see the role of passivity and self-loss in both individual and social existence, is a failure to attend to a wide expanse of human motivation, behavior, and conduct that, although intertwined with, are also practically distinct from, any number of ways of using the concept of interest.

While, as we have seen, interests spur resistance to established norms, nevertheless norms are an active factor in Niebuhr's thought. In his discussion of Augustine's political realism Niebuhr cautions against focusing exclusively on power and interest alone as the exclusive sources of human motivation. In addition to power and interest, Niebuhr argues that the human being is "a curious creature" with a powerful pull of obligation to others. In fact, so strong is this sense of obligation to people that the impulse to seek one's own interests is, Niebuhr argues, actually covered over with the pretension of serving others.[46] Likewise, in *The Nature and Destiny of Man* he states that humans are "not consistently egoistic." In an attack on the pessimism about human nature that permeates the thought of Luther and Hobbes, Niebuhr maintains that democratic societies "disprove" their pessimism, because such societies recognize the positive contribution that rules and principles of justice have to make to the quality of political and social life. But, again, Niebuhr keeps the dialectic going, cautioning that while norms are real they must not be reduced to mere "instruments of a sense of social obligation" or to "tools of egoism."[47] In other words, norms are an active factor in human motivation to be distinguished from obligation as such and not simply understood as a cover for egoism. Later in his argument he claims that all systems of justice display a tendency to place limits on everyone's interests so as to keep one person from pursuing his or her personal advantage at the expense of another. But here again, he points

---

46. Niebuhr, *ERN*, 123.
47. *NDM2*, 249.

out that "the taint of passion and self-interest" remains operative in any and every attempt of justice to calculate the rightful claims of other people.[48]

So norms play an active role in Niebuhr's thought, and an important aspect of the function of norms lies in their ability to limit self-interest. Nonetheless, the limiting function of norms operates in a larger dialectical relationship in which individuals (or nations) use norms to promote their self-interest. To lose the tension of this dialectic in Niebuhr's understanding of norms and their ability to limit *as well as* to further interests is to fail to understand the complex dynamic of their relationship in his view.

9. The Infinite Variety of Interests

The wide sweep with which interest is conceived in Niebuhr's thought is quite extraordinary. He writes of "the whole field of vital interests," of "endless variations of interests," and of "the infinite variety of the compounds of self-concern." Yet, he never develops these notions as full-fledged concepts; rather, he uses them while addressing other substantive questions. For example, he speaks of "the whole field of vital interest" in an argument against the notion of a "universal reason" or an "impartial perspective" by which this "field of interest" can be addressed. Yet even in settings designed explicitly and intentionally to be objective and impartial (i.e., courtrooms and the like), the contingent character of all human perspectives remains fundamentally inescapable. Here Niebuhr references Marxist claims that the moral objectivity "of all laws and rules of justice" amount to "rationalizations of interest" by powerful parties in societies.[49] In his language about "endless variations of interest" Niebuhr also comments about the endless ways that pursuit of interest contributes to the preservation of order and the achievement of a relative justice in modern democratic societies.[50]

Perhaps most interesting of all in Niebuhr's sweeping conception of interest is his language about "the infinite variety of self-concern." In one place he invokes this notion in a discussion of the relation between egoism and altruism in which he contends that neither of them can finally be eliminated by "one in favor of the other." Instead, the human self is a combination of both—of a concern for the self, on the one hand, and of a concern composed in part of "creative and responsible interests," on the other hand.

48. Ibid., 252.
49. Ibid.
50. *MNHC*, 61.

He argues that this combination or "compound" of egoism and altruism varies "infinitely" and can be found in those with the lowest character as well as those with the highest. Moreover, Niebuhr contends that "egoism is a fairly universal concomitant of creative efforts of all kinds." Common sense, for example, understands that human egoism is never absent in human relationships, and criticism of egoism is moderate or harsh depending upon how "vexatious" it is and the extent to which the egoistic individual engages in self-deceit or the insidious misleading of others.[51]

10. The Web of Universal or General Interests

Finally, in *Man's Nature and His Communities* Niebuhr uses the metaphor of a web to characterize "universal or general interests." He is addressing here the dialectical character of a culture's values and its national interests, with the latter eluding any simple definition because the multiple factors "of prestige, power, and force" require careful consideration. The result of this dialectic is a "complexity of the relation" that undercuts both idealistic and realistic accounts of national action, although still in basic harmony "with a moderate realism."

The significant issue for Niebuhr is that in analyses of this kind, one finds "a web of mutual and universal or general interests" to which "national interests are inextricably related." He believes that to posit exclusively a narrow interest in the context of such a web without connection to any more encompassing interests than those intrinsic or particular to it will necessarily result in its defeat.

At the same time, Niebuhr holds that the interest of the nation cannot be ignored. He characterizes the tension between these two positions as "merely a vivid reminder" that collective morality at the height of its expression must "be governed by a wise apprehension of concurrent interests, rather than by a sacrifice of the 'lower' to the ' higher' interests."[52] In other words, national interests participate in a web of mutual and universal interests. To pursue national interests to the exclusion of these more enlightened interests is self-defeating; to pursue enlightened self-interests without heed for national interests is naïve and unrealistic.

To summarize thus far, Niebuhr uses the concept of interest in at least ten rather distinct and significant ways. First, interest is a major factor,

---

51. *SDH*, 149–51.
52. *MNHC*, 79–80.

along with power, in resistance to established norms. Second, interest has a variety of internal dimensions, revealing it as multilayered rather than as a flat concept. The many distinctions Niebuhr makes in his use of the concept of interests suggest the multilayered character of this concept. Third, interest is a direct outgrowth of the existential self-regard of individuals, a dynamic that Niebuhr famously argues is compounded in group life. Fourth, Niebuhr sometimes uses the concept of interest to refer to the kinds of explicit rational calculation of advantage and gain in which individuals engage. Although there are limitations to such calculations—that is, these calculations do not stand alone, but rather constitute one aspect of what Niebuhr calls "the equilibrium of social forces"—there are also limitations in terms of the contingent and finite character of rationality *itself* as it assesses a particular individual's interests. Fifth, for Niebuhr, a significant relationship exists between self-interest and common grace, with the latter referring broadly to the way that persons and social relationships function to forestall the kind of self-destruction that occurs through an unrelieved self-seeking. For example, the affections, disciplines, and pressures that are part and parcel of familial and communal ties play creative and constructive roles in connecting the self to commitments and relationships that are larger than those of discrete, egoistic selves. Sixth, frequently Niebuhr's uses of the concept of interest call attention to its capacity for distortion. That is, for all its capacities to resist norms and elicit creativity, the distortive capacity of interest remains. This capacity of interest to produce distortion works through the self's abilities to rationalize its interests through appeal to moral values, justice, religious claims, etc., in ways that both elide and justify a fundamental self-seeking. But in this mode, "interest" refers not only to how the self deceives *others* but also to the dynamic whereby the self deceives *itself* as well (when, for example, it comes to hold an elevated estimation of its own virtue). A seventh use of the concept of interest resides in Niebuhr's phrase "the taint of interest," a phenomenon that he regards as universal and inevitable. The "taint of interest" interprets principles of justice, structures of privilege, and the framing of social situations to the advantage of one party in competition with other individuals and groups. The "taint of self-interest" means that justice is never fully perfect (i.e., objective or impartial) and never fully escapes the condition of corruption or corruptibility. Eighth, it is important in Niebuhr's use of the concept of interest to recognize that he does not see interest as the singular causal force in individual and social life. For instance, the strong sense of obligation to other human beings makes pretensions that cover self-interest with claims of service to others utterly indispensable, even if such pretensions are indeed fundamentally hypocritical. What is important to note in this hypocritical necessity is how the sense of obligation to others functions as a real causal force in social life. It may not be able to fully ameliorate the negative working and effects of interests, but it is also far from impotent or inconsequential in a reckoning of causal forces in social life. Ninth, Niebuhr writes about the infinite nature of interests—its endless variations and the apparent inexhaustible variety of the compounds of self-regard and altruism. Thus framed, it is difficult to avoid concluding that not only is there not just one definition of interest for Niebuhr, but that there cannot be even a single adequate characterization of it. Rather, Niebuhr employs a multivariant notion to address the enormously wide range of issues and settings that he treats over the course of his long career. Finally, Niebuhr uses the image of a web as a metaphor for universal or general interests. While continuing to hold to a moderate realism, he seeks to convey the complexity of the relationship between the dialectic character of a culture's values and its national interests. He points out that the pursuit of narrow interests is attended by self-defeat on account of the way that such a strategy neglects the larger web of more comprehensive, universal interests and their complex relationship to human and moral values.

QUESTIONS ABOUT NIEBUHR'S USES OF INTERESTS

Before moving on, I want to raise a few questions about these ten uses of interest Niebuhr employs. For one thing, if interest is understood as that which resists established norms, what does this do to the notion of enlightened self-interest? Clearly enlightened self-interest is not always—maybe not even usually—in conflict with established norms but in fact may be in concert with them. Is there not a need for further conceptual refinement here? Or do we just assume that the focus is to be only on narrow or selfish interests when describing resistance to established norms? The problem with this construal is that narrow self-interest can be deeply embedded in the status quo and in concert with established norms in some contexts, though I am sure Niebuhr would not regard them as universal. Niebuhr must have considered such things, but his conceptuality is not adequate to it.

Further, self-regard seems to be central to his understanding of interest, but self-regard does not always line up with rational calculation of advantage. Indeed, self-regard can overwhelm such rationality and, in fact, violate the advantage of the self. While this can certainly happen in the self-deceit of an individual or group, there is the greater problem that self-regard is not coterminous with advantage or gain. Where entire territories of the self or a group do not come into play in the calculations of advantage or the games of gain, life can lose its vitality and richness. I think here especially of people worn out with the flat rationalities of the treadmill pursuits of interest in these forms. Historically, the impulses of romanticism have fed on such dissatisfaction on no few occasions, and such impulses cannot be reduced to passions alone.

In addition, the relationship between long-term and short-term interests and wide and narrow interests seems to require either further description or additional conceptualities or both in order for Niebuhr's uses of the word *interests* to be clear. That is, at what point does long-term interest or enlightened self-interest actually become the common good? Niebuhr is alert to the fact that a narrow self-interest can be destructive of long-term interests, and he has an appreciation for the concurrence of interest between competing individuals or groups, but are these enough? Does the word *interest* have such monumental importance in his understanding of political realism that it must continue to be used so broadly even when it is neither sufficiently descriptive nor accurate enough for a more perceptive analysis of social and political forms of life?

Lastly, when one looks at the complex classifications of interest, the taint of interest, and the endless and infinite varieties of interest in Niebuhr's thought, I wonder if the word *interest* does not finally mean something as pedestrian as "what people want to do." Reduced to such a formulation, the concept of interest becomes a tautology. This is not a new problem, as we shall see in the next section; historically, interest is not a stable concept. In fact, its variations of use in the West since the late medieval period are instructive and will help us address these issues in Niebuhr's elusive use of this important concept.

Niebuhr's work with the concept of interest illustrates graphically the style of his approach to problems and issues. He virtually avoids definitions (Lovin), and he is not very precise about the framing of his thought (Rasmussen), in this case the wide use he makes of a key concept. Furthermore, if his use of interests is not equivocal (Stone), it lacks full coherence. As

Tillich says, "he just starts knowing"; and as H. Richard Niebuhr suggests, a great deal of his presuppositions lie below the surface of his exposition.

Lovin characterizes Niebuhr's work as synthetic, meaning that he connects related ideas into a complex whole, an effort that does not strictly define but rather clarifies meaning by what a concept excludes. When it comes to Niebuhr's use of interest, however, it is not so much a complex whole as a very large box of tools—all of them called by the same name. The problem is that a framing hammer is not a sledgehammer, and a chisel is not a screwdriver, but a master craftsman such as Niebuhr, while facing very different political circumstances, seems to understand how a variety of instruments of public criticism and action are to be put to use. But I find his nomenclature around the concept of interest to be not only inadequate to the range of human motivation he considers but also confusing and, finally, tautological. Yet, as I suggested in the paragraph above, the problem is not Niebuhr's alone; he has a great deal of company historically, and we turn now to that very interesting story.

ALBERT O. HIRSCHMAN ON INTEREST

Concepts do not stand still across time. It is clear that concepts change and that we can be informed by the study of their origination and the changes in their use in new places, times, and ways. This is quite true of the concept of interest. Albert O. Hirschman provides an illuminating discussion of interest in his extraordinary book *The Passions and the Interests*. In the rather spare summary that follows, I cannot hope to convey the full-bodied character of his discussion, but perhaps I can suggest something of the historical, variegated use of the concept of interest.

Hirschman's discussion begins with the downfall of the notion of glory from its privileged place in medieval codes of chivalry.[53] To oversimplify the saga of glory's eclipse, a new striving for honor—a moral virtue related to, but not quite identical with, glory—emerged in the sixteenth century, during the Renaissance. Additionally, the emergent ethos of honor that replaced the ideology of glory also coincided with the rise of a commitment to the acquisitive drive and to the behaviors and practices associated with it, especially commerce, banking, and, eventually, industry. This new complex of practices and behaviors was not the result of a triumph of one

---

53. *PI*, 10–11.

robust ideology over a rival. Rather, Hirschman shows that the real story is far more complicated and circuitous.[54]

This exaltation of glory operated at cross grain to the teaching of theologians such as Augustine, Thomas, Dante, and others who regarded it as both "vain and sinful." Nevertheless, during the sixteenth century, under the influence of the Renaissance, "the striving for honor" became "a dominant ideology," due partly to the declining influence of the church but also to aristocratic claimants who drew upon widely available Greek and Roman texts proclaiming "the pursuit of glory."[55] This story, however, does not begin with the Renaissance, nor does it come through some new set of norms for the individual. Instead, it arises in the theory of statecraft, and specifically in the instruction given to the prince to build, sustain, and extend power. The works of Machiavelli, Hobbes, and Spinoza develop a sharp distinction between the human as normatively understood, and the human as he or she "really is." Given this distinction, one task of political philosophy is to examine the human subject in terms of the actual human appetites and predilections or, in a word, *passions* (rather than solely in terms of ideal human qualities that the very "best" individuals embody). Consequently, the core issue of political philosophy became one of how to address or manage human passion.[56]

While a number of arguments were offered for the control of the passions, the idea that passions must be countered by still other passions ultimately won out.[57] The word *interest* became the umbrella term assigned to those passions identified as capable of a countervailing function.[58] In this way humans were understood as fundamentally passionate creatures, and "interest" was conceived as a particular type of passion that could counter

54. Ibid., 12.

55. Ibid., 11. Stephen Holmes, in his *Passions and Constraint*, makes an important response to Hirschman's work on the concept of interest. He argues that Hirschman's discussion of the history of self-interest is inadequate at three points: first, that Hirschman's focus on glory fails to give adequate attention to "irrational motivations" with which interests were sharply contrasted; second, Hirschman does not address the degree to which religion, especially the belief in original sin, gave rise to more positive views toward self-interest; and third, Hirschman alludes to but does not develop "the egalitarian implications of the postulate of universal self-interest." These criticisms do not, however, affect my use of Hirschman in my effort to demonstrate the highly variegated uses of the word *interest* across the last five centuries or so. Holmes, *Passions and Constraint*, 55.

56. *PI*, 13f.

57. Ibid., 20–31.

58. Ibid., 41–42.

other passions. Consequently, it was necessary to distinguish between those passions that were "tamers" and those that were "wild" and required domestication. For my purposes, it will suffice simply to say that the taming passions became identified as "interests," while the wild passions continued to be called "passions."[59]

Although the concept of interest seems to have emerged in the context of political philosophy, with the attempt to instruct princes to make sagacious decisions for their rule in contrast to being subject to passions that led them astray, such a move was also an attempt to throw off the teachings of the church and other normative claims that had become burdensome to the real world of politics. Yet, the idea of interest could weigh as heavily upon the decisions of a prince as religious or moral teaching. Furthermore, interest was not always a helpful notion, because the term *interest* itself became difficult to use, a result of the uncertainty of what it meant and therefore what was required in order to pursue it. Its potential difficulties notwithstanding, the concept of interest seemed to function quite effectively when employed to describe the self-seeking and rationality of groups or individuals within the state. In this larger domain, self-seeking and rationality became particularly relevant, even hopeful, as categories.

By the late seventeenth century, a further shift in the concept of interest became perceptible as the language of interests in relationship to groups and individuals began to take on the connotation of economic aspirations, specifically in the more limited sense of economic advantage.[60] While this conception was not uncontested, economic interests ascended to signal importance.

By the eighteenth century Adam Smith proposed the idea that the commanding motive of a human being was the "desire of bettering our condition"; Smith argued that "an augmentation of fortune is the means by which the greater part of men propose and wish to better their condition. It is the means the most vulgar and the most obvious."[61] Smith's new understanding of interest reconfigures the older dichotomy between passions and interest, so that the opposition between these two now represents something quite different than was previously the case. The result is that a grouping of passions like "greed, avarice, or love of lucre" can now be used to counteract those passions of "ambition, lust for power, or sexual

---

59 Ibid., 41.
60. Ibid., 37.
61. Smith, *Wealth of Nations*, 325, quoted in Hirschman, *PI*, 40f.

lust." Hirschman highlights a notable consequence of this reconfiguration: it elevated the quality of avarice (more commonly rendered as "greed") to a very privileged status within the notion of interest as the set of taming passions.[62] No longer was avarice understood as one of the passions in need of *taming*; in Smith's hands, avarice was reformulated as one of the *tamers*—in short, as a bona fide interest. In this way, moneymaking was no longer identified as a "passion" but took on a new role as a prosocial "interest." Concealed in *interest*—what Hirschman calls a "new, comparatively neutral, and colorless term"—avarice began again to compete with the other passions, only now it was relieved of the stigma of the old epithets. Indeed, the classification of avarice as "interest" bestowed on moneymaking "a positive and curative connotation."[63]

Yet not everyone readily accepted the centrality of interest in human motivation. The emergent notion of interests and passions came under fire from the likes of Shaftesbury and Bishop Butler, who held that interest was much more complicated by the passions. Their thought rehabilitated the passions as "the essence of life and as a potentially creative force."[64] If previously the passions were turbulent forces in need of control by moderating passions called "interests," now passions, too, were given a positive valence. Passions were said to make the world a better place (as opposed to one ruled by interest alone). With interest having been narrowed down to mere material advantage, this conception of passions flourished in the place carved out for creativity and expressivity.[65]

But if Shaftesbury's and Butler's critiques contributed to a more positive conception of passion, interest conceived as moneymaking came to be placed in a positive frame by others. In particular, commerce came to be seen as antithetical to violence, as captured by the phrase "the *douceur* of commerce." Hirschman explains that *douceur*, while not easily translatable, connotes "sweetness, softness, calm, and gentleness and is the antonym

---

62. Ibid., 41.

63. Ibid., 41–42.

64. Ibid., 47.

65. Nevertheless, interests brought two ingredients to make for an orderly world: predictability and constancy. To know that others will pursue their interests brings a certain predictability and transparency to human affairs, and confidence in this kind of foresight gave the world, especially the economic conduct of individuals, constancy. "The by-product of individuals acting predictably in accordance with their economic interests was therefore not an uneasy *balance*, but a strong *web* of interdependent relationships." Smith, *Wealth of Nations*, quoted in Hirschman, *PI*, 51–52. Smith's italics.

of violence."[66] Jacques Savary was the first to describe commerce as "this continuous exchange of all comforts of life"; he further claimed that "commerce makes for all the gentleness [*douceur*] of life." Indeed, even Montesquieu observed "wherever there is commerce, there the ways of men [sic] are gentle."[67] Others stated that commerce "softens and polishes the manners of man [sic]."[68]

During the eighteenth century, new currents of thought continued to sweep across Europe. It was argued that some passions are less wild and harmful than others; others could even be beneficial. Thus there developed a sharp distinction between "benign and malignant passions,"[69] a distinction that, through the eighteenth century, became the equivalent of that previously noted between interests and passions in the seventeenth century. By means of variations on this theme of benign and malignant passions, moneymaking—moderately pursued—came to be understood as a "natural affection." While its excessive pursuit continued to be regarded as an "unnatural" propensity, its engagement in moderation could lead to both public and private good.[70]

One problem remained: the distinction between benign and wild passions made it difficult to imagine that calm passions could prevail over the more violent proclivities. Into this debate stepped David Hume, who distinguished between calm and weak passions, as well as violent and strong ones. On the basis of Hume's distinctions, the rational, calculated pursuit and acquisition of wealth as a calm passion could also be quite strong and therefore victorious over any number of stormier, but nevertheless weak, passions.[71]

Glossing over any number of important developments in and elaborations on the concept of interest during the eighteenth entury, we would be remiss not to take account of Adam Smith's contributions to how this

---

66. Hirschman, *PI*, 59.

67. Ibid., 60.

68. Ibid., 61. Hirschman points out that not only does such talk seem strange to our ears, but even more so when we consider that the slave trade was quite prominent at this time, and that trade, even more broadly considered, was undeniably a risky and hazardous pursuit. But, perhaps, when compared with the alternative (one thinks of the marauding of armies and the violent treachery of the pirates of that time), the picture of the trader and his work as *douceur* gathered importance. Ibid., 62f.

69. Ibid., 63.

70. Ibid., 65.

71. Ibid., 66.

Human Nature, Interest, and Power

notion evolved. Whereas many of the thinkers Hirschman treats in his text emphasized the political effects of the pursuit of interest, Smith's *Wealth of Nations* is notable for how it provided "a powerful economic justification for the untrammeled pursuit of individual self-interest."[72] In Smith's view, it was not the case that a rising capitalism would necessarily meliorate political rule through restraint of the turbulent passions. In fact, Smith's argument cut the ground out from under such views. As we have seen, *The Wealth of Nations* presents human motivation as defined by the desire for betterment. On the one hand, this is a reductionist view of human motivation, but it is, nevertheless, not the result of Smith's being out of touch with the great range of passions. Indeed, *The Theory of Moral Sentiments* represents a significant treatise on precisely this topic. In that book Smith contends, "From whence . . . arises the emulation which runs through all the different ranks of men [sic], and what are the advantages which we propose by that great purpose of human life which we call bettering our condition? To be observed, to be attended to, to be taken notice of with sympathy, complacency, and appreciation, are all the advantages which we can propose to derive from it. It is the vanity, not the ease or the pleasure, which interests us."[73]

Here Smith's reductionist move is clearly displayed: no longer is the impulse for economic advantage autonomous, or freestanding. Rather, Smith describes this impulse as a means for the "desire for consideration"—to be taken into account, to be noticed. These are distinctly *noneconomic* desires. And yet, argues Hirschman, no matter how strong and forceful the noneconomic urges of life may be, in Smith's thought these are now made to fuel the economic desires and can only fortify these material desires, having lost their independence from them.[74]

---

72. Ibid., 100. Hirschman's italics.

73. Ibid., 108. Stephen Holmes challenges Hirschman's assessment of Adam Smith's view of interest as reductionistic. While he agrees that the concept of interest became "progressively more narrow and specialized" in the seventeenth and eighteenth centuries—at first meaning "any rational style of behavior"—it later "came to refer exclusively to moneymaking." During this same time, however, the concept took on so broad a meaning that it became a tautology, that is, referring to most anything humans want to pursue. Holmes argues that Smith used the concept in both ways—in fact, that he "alternated dizzyingly between these two claims." Holmes maintains that this "paradoxical development" is the key to understanding "the secret history of the concept." *Passions and Constraint*, 62–63.

74. Smith, *Wealth of Nations*, quoted in Hirschman, *PI*, 109.

Thus two things happen. First, noneconomic motives wind up being placed in the service of the human effort to improve one's *material* condition. With noneconomic drives now the source of economic action, Smith can give his full concentration to economic activities. The second and more significant consequence is that impulses such as "ambition, lust for power, the desire for respect" can now be slaked by economic satisfactions. No longer must passions be countered by passions, or interests serve to restrain the passions. Rather, as Hirschman points out, passions and interests are virtually one in Smith's thought.[75] These two concepts, "interests" and "passions," which in the one hundred and fifty years preceding Smith were distinct, Smith suddenly uses as synonyms.[76] Indeed, his focus, not confined to rulers or the aristocracy, is the great mass of humanity. Hirschman notes that as a result of the impact of Smith's ideas, much scholarly and political debate takes as its point of departure Smith's contention that the general welfare of the social body is best served by permitting each individual to pursue his or her material self-interest.

In his *Rival Views of Market Society* (1986), Hirschman explores the intellectual currents that characterize the nineteenth century. Although opposition to the doctrine of interest was vocal and strong, the growing importance of economics as a new scientific discipline meant that the doctrine of interest maintained high valuation. James Mill, for example, uses the assumption of rational self-interest as the basis for articulating the first economic theory of politics. His presupposition that self-interest is necessarily rational makes it necessary for Mill to distinguish a citizen's real interests from false interests. Seizing on this distinction, Thomas B. Macaulay dismisses Mill's position as "empty," arguing that if "interest" "means only that men [sic], if they can, will do as they choose . . . [then] it is . . . idle to attribute any importance to a proposition which, when interpreted, means only that a man [sic] had rather do what he would rather do." In short, Macaulay critiques Mill's view of interest as essentially a tautology.[77] As more parties jump into the fray of defining and elaborating "interest," the concept takes on more specific uses and further shadings. Hence distinctions such as narrow self-interest, or long-term interests, or enlightened self-interest, etc., make the concept even more complex, ambiguous, and, finally, diluted.

75. Ibid., 109–10.
76. Ibid., 111.
77. *RVMS*, 48.

The concept of interest is further attenuated as the sharp distinction between passions and interest that characterized earlier conceptions begins to lessen. Weakened, too, is the older distinction between calm and wild passions. Hirschman speculates that this weakening can be attributed to the newer association of "interests" with moneymaking. As a result, interests come to cover virtually the entire range of human actions, from the narrowly self-centered to the sacrificially altruistic, from the prudently calculated to the passionately compulsive. In the end, interest can be said to stand behind anything people do or wish to do. Thus, to explain human action with reference to interest turns into the vacuous tautology announced by Macaulay.[78]

By the end of the nineteenth century, much philosophical, psychological, and sociological thought had become entranced by the role of the nonrational—that is, what can be characterized as "the instinctual-intuitive, the habitual, the unconscious, the ideologically and neurotically driven" in human affairs. Consequently, the distance between the disciplines of philosophy, psychology, and sociology on the one hand, and the field of economics on the other, increases as economic thought, so myopically based on the rational, calculating, self-interested individual, is not able to incorporate these new learnings into the formalistic and positivistic frame of its discipline.[79]

With respect to more recent trends in the twentieth century, Hirschman reports "signs of discontent with the progressive evisceration of the concept of interest," understood as a narrow, rational pursuit of material gain by individuals.[80] Conservatives reaffirmed the "orthodox meaning of interest" and called into question the concept of enlightened self-interest, believing that the wisest course of action was to stay with a narrow conception of self-interest. Others reject the idea that human conduct and behavior can be accounted for by interest so regarded. They understand that action can be motivated by a range of noninstrumental factors such as altruism, ethical commitments, concern for the public interest, etc. Therefore, they discard conceptions of interest that see such conduct as nothing more than forms of concealed self-interest in the more narrow sense. Furthermore, this "noninstrumental behavior" that interest motivates takes on considerable variation in its forms of expression. Here Hirschman seems to have in

78. Ibid., 50.
79. Ibid., 51.
80. Ibid.

mind, for example, the level of participation in public and political affairs that fluctuates greatly in different types of governments and societies, from the suppression of oppressive states to the apathy of more open ones.[81]

Finally, Hirschman observes that a society in which the individual simply pursues his or her rational, calculated self-interest where the public interest is served indirectly "becomes a reality only under holy nightmarish political conditions! More civilized political circumstances necessarily imply a less transparent and less predictable society." He concludes that the most predictable thing about human affairs is their unpredictability, and so to attempt to reduce human action to a single motive such as interest, regardless of how interest is conceived, is futile.[82]

To sum up Hirschman's story of the concept of interest in the West, it is clear that the concept travels through great changes in its definitions and uses. Its relationship to the passions, for example, is itself quite various, and its relationship to the whole notion of rational calculation is troubled, to say the least. Further, the characterization of interests as douceur hardly squares with the rapacious role interests can play according to yet other designations of the concept in the West. Certainly, there are those who question the whole notion that human motivation can be attributed to one thing—i.e., interests—and there are important moves in the West to challenge the kind of flat rationalities that would reduce human impulses to advantage and gain. What we do not find in the West, however, is some essential, universal notion of interest. Rather, unless the concept is carefully and precisely used, it operates as a tautology. Before returning to the implications of Hirschman's work for the thought of Reinhold Niebuhr on interest, I must first consider the work of William E. Connolly.

WILLIAM E. CONNOLLY ON INTEREST

William E. Connolly is widely known as a theorist and writer in the fields of democracy and pluralism. Influenced by William James, Nietzsche, Gilles Deleuze, and Felix Guattari, he brings to his work a new conceptuality and expands the categories by which politics and human motivation can be understood. In his writing he analyzes the alliance of "cowboy capitalism" and conservative evangelical Christianity using a new range of categories. He rejects the usual search for things like common economic interests between

81. Ibid., 52.
82. Ibid., 53.

Republican conservatives and right-wing Christians or through some ideological manipulation of the latter by the former.[83]

Connolly's analysis includes and develops a number of categories that are quite relevant to our discussion of interests. For instance, one of the questions Connolly considers at length is why so many working-class whites adopt what he calls a "militant politics of individual aspiration," which leads them to identify with higher socioeconomic classes (of which they are not likely ever to be a part) rather than with the class of which they now are a part. In other words, why do working-class whites not follow their class interests?[84] I will not attempt to summarize his larger discussion, which deserves careful attention, but will focus on Connolly's treatment of what he terms "the politics of identity." The "politics of identity" are relevant to our discussion of interest because Connolly says that this politics "both infiltrates and nudges the expression of self-interest."[85] In fact, this politics seems to override the self-interest and economic interest of working-class whites.

A particularly salient concept in Connolly's analysis is that of what he calls the capitalist-evangelical assemblage or alliance. As we see above, this assemblage resonates with a significant segment of people in contemporary U.S. politics. He argues that an important effect of this assemblage is the emergence and extraordinarily effective operation of a powerful "resonance machine." Connolly's "resonance machine" is a politico-socio-economic force—a "real force," he insists—virtually a "sort of contagion" that pulls "some constituencies more than others toward a theo-economic spirituality."[86] That is, manifold elements such as corporate capitalism, evangelical Christians, the media, and the Republican Party infiltrate into each other and become a moving complex in which they join and vibrate in their interinfluence and interinvolvement. In this sense they become a kind of echo chamber of reverberating impacts, each affecting the others. The result is a qualitative coming together that cannot be adequately accounted for by more classical means of analysis and explanation, such as self-interest and ideological machinations.

This notion of a "capitalist-evangelical resonance machine" provides a basis for Connolly to elaborate a number of factors (over and above that of

83. *CCAS*, xi.
84. Ibid., 149 n. 21.
85. Ibid., xi.
86. Ibid., 42.

just "interest") that shape human motivation. One characteristic of the capitalist-evangelical resonance machine that Connolly treats at some length is that of a shared "spiritual disposition to existence" or an ethos that is marked by what he calls "ruthless, ideological extremism." This extremism stands at the ready to "defend neoliberal ideology" in spite of compelling evidence of its limits and problems. Further, this extremist commitment will "create or condone scandals" to oppose any party who stands in opposition to them. Connolly maintains that such commitments represent "a fundamental disposition toward the world."[87]

Connolly's argument is not that this ethos *causes* any particular behavior(s) on the part of its adherents, but rather that this ethos is one of the elements of the patterns of reverberation with others. As he says, this ethos "infiltrates, inflects, and intensifies a host of perceptions, institutionalized creeds, economic interests, alliances, loyalties, enmities, and political priorities. Each of these encoded elements in turn recoils back upon the ethos, modifying it in this way and intensifying it in that. The cumulative result is a resonance machine, not a windup doll."[88]

Connolly further clarifies that this general ethos, as an "existential orientation," encourages this alliance to "transfigure interest into greed, greed into anti-market ideology, anti-market ideology into market manipulation, market manipulation into state institutionalization of those operations, and the entire complex into policies to pull the security net away from ordinary workers, consumers, and retirees—some of whom are then set up to translate new intensities of resentment and cynicism into participation in the machine."[89]

Most significantly, people formed by this kind of spirituality together cultivate the development of alliances with others who share similar "spiritual affinities,"[90] thereby perpetuating the cycle and expanding the sphere of influence of its sensibilities.

For Connolly, an important factor in the ability of the capitalist-evangelical assemblage's resonance machine to draw people from and unite them across a host of differences—differences in religion, social class, everyday

---

87. Ibid., 42.

88. Ibid., 42. Connolly is also not suggesting that anyone who believes in a deregulated economy necessarily participates in this alliance, its resonance character, and its existential ethos. Many do not.

89. Ibid., 43

90. Ibid.

life settings, etc.—is "the *intensity* of the ethos," which is its defining mark. This intensity is such that any group that stands in opposition to the sensibilities of this ethos encounters severe rebuke and blame. As an example of how this intensity works, Connolly recalls the claim by Bill Clinton that the Republican Party contains "a destruction machine." Yet, Connolly asserts that Clinton's characterization of this ethos as specifically that of the Republican Party is too narrow, arguing that "the destruction machine" Clinton identified exceeds the lines drawn by the dominant political parties in the United States to include various new corporate practices as well.[91] Connolly does not name these "new corporate practices" at this point, but I understand him to mean the participation of some corporations in this bellicose ethic, in support of extreme right-wing think tanks, related media, and in financing extremist groups like the Tea Party.

Connolly draws on the work of political economist Mark Blyth, particularly Blyth's account of the rejection of Keynesianism in the 1970s and 1980s and its replacement by supply-side economics. In Blyth's account, supply-side economics is a distinctive set of economic ideas taken up and promoted by right-wing think tanks, promulgated to the public through the media, initially accepted in a limited manner by President Carter, and then later embraced completely by President Reagan. Yet Blyth maintains that the shift from Keynesianism to supply-side economics cannot be adequately accounted for either by "structural determinants" *or* by "the fixed economic interests" of the people who adopt these views.[92] Blyth observes that in times of economic insecurity some agents have a greater capacity than others to make their ideas known. Consequently, these agents play a crucial and compelling role in how people come to understand and relate to their political commitments and economic interests. Blyth works with the question of why certain economic ideas take on more significance during such periods, particularly in cases when the explanatory capacity of those ideas is relatively weak, like those of supply-side economics. He contends that when people are not clear about their interests, they are more likely to respond to avenues of action that are more in keeping with their "core identities" (i.e., the kind of people they think they are or understand themselves to be)[93] than those that are more in keeping with their *actual*

---

91. Ibid.

92. Ibid., 45. Quotes in this paragraph are Connolly's.

93. These core identities are a mix of "faith, doctrine, and sensibility." These are "affect-imbued ideas" which form their core identities and take up residence in "the soft

economic and political interests as such. What is crucial for our purposes is the way that, in effect, Blyth identifies a major qualification of how interests are followed—or, really, *not* followed—by the impact of think tanks and the media, conditions of economic insecurity, and a subsequent turn to core identities. The work of Blyth on the politics of identity thus adds yet another dimension to the range of categories explored by Connolly in developing a more descriptive account of the relationship and dynamics of conservative evangelical Christianity and right-wing capitalism.

My point here is not to posit the existence of some "universal" dynamic whereby people are drawn inexorably to ignore their self-interest, variously understood, in times of uncertainty and to turn instead to issues of their core identities that are deeply embedded in the tissues of their bodies in some essentialist fashion. To the contrary, I am suggesting that this dynamic Blyth identifies has compelling descriptive power in our time. To be clear, I do not and would not generalize this dynamic across all times and places. At the same time, this dynamic that Blyth so vividly depicts suggests that it is important to pay attention to *particular* contexts, to the *specific* relationships and, yes, the *power arrangements* that are at work in any time and place. High generalizations imposed on "history" are not helpful to the extent that they obscure too many specific dynamics and forces.

At the same time, we are also remiss to identify "interest" as the key category (along with power—although I get ahead of myself here) to understand resistance to established norms or, for that matter, as the most important concept for the analysis of a social setting. Following Hirschman, the concept of interest is too loaded with a history of variegated—and finally tautological—use to be able to clarify the set of social dynamics that most needs to be brought into focus and understood.

Parenthetically, let me say in criticism of Connolly that while I find his description of the resonance machine, the existential ethos, the spiritual affinities, and so on quite suggestive, each of these needs far greater exploration in terms of the concrete discourses, the explicit practices, and the right-wing movement and institutional ways of thinking and acting that are identified in concepts like these. Otherwise they become quite abstract, quite ephemeral, even spectral.

---

tissues of affect, emotion, habit, and posture, as well as the upper reaches of the intellect."

CONCLUSION

In this chapter I have pointed to ten ways in which Niebuhr uses the concept of interest in the corpus of his written work, ranging from self-regard to the rational calculation of advantage, from a concept that resists established norms to an infinite range of uses that include the most common or universal interests. Without rehashing each of these ten modes of interest again, I think it suffices simply to say that there is no small range of uses of the word *interests*, and it is for this reason that I must confess that I find that such an apparently limitless use of the concept finally engages Niebuhr in a tautology.

Hirschman's survey of the history of the concept of interest in the last five hundred years or so in the West clarifies how it is that Niebuhr could use the term *interest* in so many different ways without perceiving this variety to be problematic (let alone vacuous). Any suggestion that "interest" has a set or essential meaning is deeply challenged by this history of the concept. While Niebuhr at no point makes such an essentialist claim about "interest," the great prominence the concept has in his thought simply must, for this reason, be called into question. If "interest" is not finally a tautology in Niebuhr's thought, then it requires significant reconceptualization in terms of the very usages to which he puts the term. As it is, it will not do.

In chapter 1 I draw from Connolly's work the idea that not only our subjectivity but also our intersubjectivity as well, functions on a number of registers besides those of the conscious and the rational with no little variation. Such variation clearly indicates that political life and thought—indeed, a great range of life and thought—operates on the basis of layered intricacies of our personal and social subjectivities, rather than straightforwardly on one or the other. Connolly highlights how even our more careful, "conceptually refined thinking" is shaped by such layers. These layers function with a density and an intensity that cannot and, indeed, *must not* be ignored, either in politics or in other dimensions of our lives. Connolly's treatment of Blyth points toward the role that identity plays in shaping an individual's or group's understanding of their interests and, by extension, their pursuits thereof. In short, Connolly's work complicates any social, political, or theological thought that would give self-interest an overly central role in understanding human motivation and in analyzing human conduct and behavior. To be sure, Niebuhr names vitalities, unconscious factors, passions, etc., in his work, but the work of Connolly opens up a considerable array of suggestive concepts—when based in concrete practices of a discursive and nondiscursive kind—that push past more abstract labels like the unconscious, vitalities, and the passions.

While these thinkers come long after Niebuhr's death, and he of course cannot be held accountable for such developments in social thought, nevertheless we must address them. Even more problematic views of human nature such as Niebuhr's that focus primarily on binary conceptualizations like transcendence and finitude or forms and vitalities tend to approach the complexities of subjects and intersubjectivities too simplistically. Binary conceptions—even when as brilliantly formulated as Niebuhr's—focus attention too narrowly and impose ideas comprised of too few options. Binary concepts and their limitations are thus given too central an explanatory role, one that is inadequate to comprehend fully the great range of human action and motivation. If, as I argue in chapter 1, Niebuhr's view of human nature can divert our attention from some of the most important features of a given political context, his overreliance of the concept of self-interest, variously used, similarly obscures an enormous range of factors at work in human communities. In the light of what we have seen, it is far better to take a more exacting look at what is going on, resisting the temptation to impose a prefabricated "universal" or "primordial" set of categories on the complexities of a form of life.

To clarify one last time, it is not my point that we should now develop a systematic theory of human motivation composed of carefully defined concepts of different kinds of self-interest and layers of subjectivity. I see the ideas of different kinds of self-interests and layers of subjectivity rather as an opening to the *specifics* of the dynamics that are at work in the complex, historically contingent, intersubjective, and relational forces that together constitute the ethos and social landscape in and of a given time and place.

Also, I do understand that, as the saying goes, "We all come from somewhere," and this condition of "coming from somewhere" means that we cannot but bring assumptions, concepts, and practice-formed bodies to the things we do. My contention here is that we need to work to stay open to the complexity of various contexts. We must not narrow the range of our attention prematurely with concepts that are too simple in their "universality," too various in their usages, or so abstract in their conceptualization that they are reductionist in their application and distortive in their descriptive power.

With these thoughts in place we are now ready to turn to Niebuhr's understanding of power.

3

Niebuhr's Concept of Power

I HAVE CHALLENGED REINHOLD Niebuhr's view of human nature and offered an alternative one, not a constituting self but a subject constituted in the discourses and practices of a specific form or forms of life. Such a subject becomes an agent by means of linguistic and institutional networks that establish and form specific modes of connecting to people, to objects, and to one's self. In these terms a subject-agent is not reducible to the binary dynamics of Niebuhr's existential self. Instead, a far more complex reflexivity, different concepts of limitations, and various layers of subjectivity and intersubjectivity are at work in the introspective practices of given forms of life. In addition, Niebuhr's too central focus on self-interest—especially when used as variously as he does—loses exactness in its descriptive power. It obscures a far greater range of human motivation, behavior, and conduct and must finally be classified as a tautology. In his uses of the concept of interest, Niebuhr participates in a long history in the West where this concept has never been stable. This brings us to a third foundational set of concepts—Niebuhr's understanding of power and the balance of power.

THE CONCEPT OF POWER

To begin, it is clear in Niebuhr that power is not in and of itself evil. In his essay "The Power and Weakness of God," Niebuhr argues that "the goodness of power" is closely connected to the entire "'non-spiritual' interpretation of life." The Christian faith, with its refusal to abstract the spiritual from the more "dynamic stuff of life," does not call the spiritual good and life's dynamic energies evil, but rather, the whole of the creation is good, as Niebuhr says: "All forms of creation represent various strategies of power." So power participates in the creation, derives from its ultimate source in God, and is good.[1]

Power is, however, always in danger of becoming unjust and evil. The inequalities and the coercion of power operate in human affairs so that one person, party, group, nation, etc., can always take advantage of, exploit, oppress, and violate those lacking sufficient power to resist these human propensities in social life. As Niebuhr states, "Power is not evil in itself; but evil incarnates itself in power and cannot finally be defeated without the use of power."[2] In this sense, power is morally neutral. Ronald Stone observes that, on Niebuhr's view, power is in essence "the vitality of human life and is almost synonymous with energy."[3] Here power is bound up with the vitalities of human being as both spirit and nature.

Niebuhr maintains that as a unity and interrelation of the spiritual and the physical, human nature generates "an endless variety and types of power, from that of pure reason to . . . pure physical force."[4] With a claim like this it is clear that Niebuhr's conception of power is not strictly reductive, that is, it cannot be reduced to coercion. He regards physical force as "always a last resort in individual relations"; and regarding civilized relations he states that these are "governed more by spiritual, than by physical, facets of power." Remember here that Niebuhr sees vitalities as one dimension of the self with form being the other, as we saw in chapter 1. For Niebuhr human vitalities are constituted of the energies of both nature and spirit: by the energies of our nature he means the physical urges and appetites of our bodies; by the vitalities of our spirit he means the dynamics of our imagination and reason, but also that our freedom issues in yearnings that emerge from our capacity to envision new possibilities. The human self combines all of these. He points out that one person can hold another in slavery by means of "mental and emotional energy, the possession or the pretension of virtue, the prestige of an heroic life, or of a gentle birth." Niebuhr is quick to say, however, that spiritual power is "not, for that reason, naturally more just."[5]

1. *ERN*, 24.
2. Ibid., 25.
3. *RNPP*, 176.
4. *NDM*2, 260
5. Ibid., 261.

It should be noted here that for Niebuhr power is understood as a possession. He often writes of the way in which people guard their power and how "the very possession of power and prestige" inevitably involves intrusions upon the power and prestige of others.[6] In another example he discusses those circumstances in which an individual or a group, including the nation, "possesses undue power."[7] In yet another example he addresses "the possession of power" and the responsibilities attendant to it.[8] Since I will challenge the notion of power as a possession, I register this concept of power as possession here.

From time to time, Niebuhr provides lists of types of power, but I agree with Stone that Niebuhr was less interested in carefully cataloging all the forms power takes than he was in underscoring the basic point of power's boundless range and innumerable potential configurations.[9] In this connection, Niebuhr argues that "on the whole social power rests upon differentiations of social function." Here he lists the soldier, the priest, and economic and political power as examples of different forms of social power. As I read this passage, Niebuhr is not attempting to construct a comprehensive list of types of social power. Rather, his point is that the kinds of social power involved in these four examples indicate the variety of ways in which social power can be configured and can function.[10]

In this discussion of economic and political power, Niebuhr challenges the modern contention that economic power is the most basic type of power, and that all other forms of power derive from it. He observes that prior to the modern era economic power certainly was not the most basic form of power; clearly, it originated from other forms of power. He points out that "the first landlords were soldiers and priests who used military and religious forms of social power to possess and to acquire land." Economic power followed from military and social power, not the other way around. Moreover, while economic power contributed to the comforts that rulers enjoyed and to their preeminence across the generations, they did not derive their initial standing from it. It was only in the bourgeois period of the

---

6. *CLCD*, 20.
7. "Why the Christian Church Is Not Pacifist," in *ERN*, 116.
8. "Power and Justice," 10.
9. *RNPP*, 178.
10. *NDM*2, 261.

modern era that economic power took on a more fundamental role and was thus dominant over other types of power.[11]

Stone points out that one of the central ways in which Niebuhr understood power is, as Stone puts it, "as a necessary expression of social organization and cohesion." In other words, organized power is necessary to forestall social chaos.[12] This is evident in Niebuhr's statement that "all social life represents a field of vitality, elaborated in many forms, which are related to each other in terms of both mutual support and potential conflict." He states further that "a task of conscious political contrivance in human history is to mitigate conflict and to invent instruments for the enlarging mutualities of social existence."[13] In Niebuhr's view, social harmony is not only a function of the effective rule of law, but law has primarily a negative, or restraining, function, and on the merits of its own power cannot coerce the vitalities of life. For Niebuhr, then, rather than being rooted in law, social harmony rises from the interaction between "normative conceptions of morality and law," on the one hand, and "the existing and developing forces and vitality of the community," on the other. Thus, social harmony is an interactive effect, and the social order of communities resides in the relative stability, or uncertainty, of the harmonies of human vital capacities.[14]

To sum up thus far, Niebuhr understood power theologically within the context of a fundamentally good creation. While he acknowledged unjust and evil power, he did not see injustice, coercion, or even evil itself as power's fundamental or most essential dynamic. He saw power as something like energy and, on this basis, conceived of power as acquiring and proliferating its dynamism and vitality through constant creative interaction—that is, in motion rather than from a static state or fundamentally repressive nature.

THE WILL TO POWER

The problem of power for Niebuhr comes at the point of the human will and pride. The will to power, understood as the desire to possess power, grows out of pride. Therefore the will to power always results from sin, on his view. Niebuhr names four forms of pride—power, knowledge,

11. Ibid., 261–62.
12. *RNPP*, 176
13. *NDM2*, 265.
14. Ibid., 257.

virtue, and a fourth, nonspecific form: spiritual. Niebuhr discusses two basic forms of power as pride. One of these can be called "the pride of the strong." Niebuhr associates the pride of the strong with those who assume "self-sufficiency and self-mastery" and who see themselves as being "secure against all vicissitudes."[15] The primary mark of such individuals or groups is a refusal to recognize their weakness. Such arrogant pretension can be found, at least in an incipient form, throughout all of human life, but it finds its greatest expression among people and classes who are established in a society and possess a disproportionate amount of social power. Put another way, this is the power of entitlement. Intimately connected to this form of the pride of power is the lust for power. In this lust the insecure ego—which, even among the strong, sees itself as insufficiently important or revered or feared—attempts to shore up, enhance, and secure its standing in nature or in society.[16]

Niebuhr argues that the lust for power is commonly expressed in human attempts to dominate and exploit nature. In such cases, the appropriate use of human freedom and mastery in the world devolves into "mere exploitation of nature." Human self-conceit and a misplaced sense of disdainful independence corrode "reverent gratitude toward the miracle of nature's perennial abundance." Niebuhr calls such arrogant exploitation and distorted autonomy greed, and he argues that greed is a unique expression of humanity's "inordinate ambition to hide [their] insecurity in nature."[17]

Human insecurity, however, does not grow merely from the world of nature, but from "the uncertainties of society and history." This leads to the second form that power assumes as pride. Niebuhr associates this second form of power with people who are more obviously threatened by insecurity—those who lack avenues for social recognition, for example, or whose lives are beset by economic instability or even by poor physical health.[18] Such individuals pursue this form of power as compensation for their very real vulnerability. In these cases, the pretentious arrogation of power to the self attempts to mask and compensate for profound insecurity.

---

15. *NDM*1, 188.

16. Ibid., 189.

17. Niebuhr further argues that the modern era is especially guilty of the sin of greed as will to power. Modern technology tempts present-day people to exaggerate the possibilities and the appropriateness of eliminating human vulnerability in nature: "Greed has thus become the besetting sin of bourgeois culture." Ibid., 191.

18. Ibid., 190.

Crucially, Niebuhr believes it to be "natural" for the self to attempt to evade both social and natural insecurity and to seek to do so through power over others and power over nature. If the danger of human rivalry is understood as being mitigated by the subordination of threatening others, and that greater power can guard against the enmity generated by such domination, the inevitable result is that the will to power exacerbates the insecurity it seeks to eradicate and renders the self complicit in injustice. The security it pursues resides well beyond "the limits of human finiteness," and its unruly ambition instigates apprehensions and animosities not known or confronted even in "the world of pure nature" with its impulsive competitions for survival.[19]

THE WILL TO SURVIVE AND THE WILL TO SELF-REALIZATION

In *The Children of Light and the Children of Darkness,* Niebuhr addresses the will to power and the will to self-realization in relationship to what he calls "the will to survive." Niebuhr describes the will to survive as "a natural survival impulse" that resides at the very heart of human ambition. This survival impulse is intimately bound up with both the desire to fulfill human potential (the will to self-realization) and the will to power. These Niebuhr identifies as the two forms of the "spiritualization" of the will to survive, meaning, I take it, those forms of human nature related to the transcendent capacities of the self. The first of these is the "desire to fulfill the potentialities of life." Here Niebuhr observes that humans are never satisfied simply to sustain their existence; instead, humans are "bound to seek the realization of [their] true nature." In this way, the will to live is "transmuted into the will to self-realization." For Niebuhr, the will to survive is the will to live a *human*, not simply an *animal*, existence. He maintains that self-realization, as the telos of human life, occurs through self-giving, and that it is only in self-giving that true fulfillment of the self occurs.[20]

The will to power is the second form of the spiritualization of the will to survive. In this sense, the will to power expresses the human desire for power and glory. The connection between the will to power and the will to survive rests on how physical survival alone is not adequate to human desires. Beyond survival, humans seek to gain "prestige and social approval."

19. Ibid., 192.
20. CLCD, 19.

Human Nature, Interest, and Power

Part and parcel of the human capacity to make an object of the self is the concomitant "intelligence to anticipate the perils" that await them in both nature and history. The ability to anticipate perils drives humans to pursue security against these dangers by strengthening their individual and collective power. But even further, Niebuhr argues that humans' "darkly unconscious sense" of their "insignificance in the total scheme of things" produces an arrogant pretension that is actually an attempt to compensate for this insignificance. His point is that despite what they may sometime seem to be, dynamics such as these make human conflict about more than survival alone. These social conflicts are efforts to guard the power and prestige of one individual or group against those of another in competitions for power fueled by pride. Yet, because possessing power and prestige always treads in some way on the power and prestige of others, the tendency of these conflicts is to become more layered and more intractable, more willful and more difficult than competitions in nature, where all that is at stake is survival. Moreover, Niebuhr notes that the cruelty that attends such conflicts is amplified in human group life far more than it is among individuals.[21]

With this understanding in place, we can see that the survival impulse expressed in "the will to live truly and the will to power" presents what are two different and, actually, contradictory spiritualized forms. Such fundamental contradiction is thus intractable in individual and group life. As an organic creature, a human being cannot fulfill the self apart from relation to others. Yet humans are inevitably caught in the struggles for power and prestige that result from insecurity and their pretentious compensations, delusions, and overreach. In this sense human beings are living contradictions, and the impulses of the will to live and the will to power are, as Niebuhr explains, "mixed and compounded with each other on every level of human life."[22] For this reason, Niebuhr also insists that "simple distinctions between good and evil, between selfishness and altruism" do not, finally, hold up. The will to power "inevitably justifies itself" by cloaking itself in the more acceptable will to self-realization, claiming that human life is enriched in the pursuit of directions that cover the power and interest of one party or group to the exclusion of another. Thus we have here an inevitable mixture of a justifiable survival impulse and will to self-realization

---

21. Ibid., 20–21.
22. Ibid., 21–22.

corrupted by pride and the will to power with their arrogance and distortions in service of the self in group life.

To summarize, the will to power is both a direct form and an indirect instrument of sinful pride. At its heart, the human will to power is an exhibition of human insecurity that arises among the strong and the weak alike. It is found among those who seem to have the most guarantees of protection and safety, but it is also found among those who have the least. In this way, human beings are "betrayed" by both their strength and their vulnerability, so that, as Niebuhr puts it, "there is no level of greatness and power in which the lash of fear is not at least one strand in the whip of ambition."[23] The lust for power that the will to power expresses seeks security from threats of nature as well as from the uncertainties of society and history. In the former, it arises in the attempt to dominate and exploit nature, and in the latter, to secure oneself or one's group against the threats of others. Finally, drawing on the will to survive, the will to power takes the form of two types of spiritualization—the will to self-realization and the desire for power and glory. The result is an ineradicable contradiction. Conscious of the dangers faced in human existence, the will to power is the pursuit that attempts to guarantee human significance against the towering indifference of nature and history. In turn, these pursuits exacerbate the conflicts of the will to survive. In their encroachment on the will to power of others, pursuits motivated by the ineluctable will to power render the resulting conflicts ever more irresolvable, stubborn, and beset with difficulty.

A CRITIQUE OF NIEBUHR'S VIEW OF POWER

The complexities of power in Niebuhr's view are enormous. The forms or types of power operate at every level of personal, familial, communal, or societal life, as well at the international level. My concern with Niebuhr's approach to power, especially in its connection with human vitalities, is that it needs conceptual refinement not only in terms of the concept of power itself but, as we shall see later, in the concept of the balance of power. I recognize that Niebuhr might well have been restive with such conceptual interests given his impatience for or lack of attention to definitions and more exact characterizations of terms, but the conceptual refinement needed concerns substantive matters, politically and otherwise, as I shall demonstrate.

23. *NDM*1, 194.

Human Nature, Interest, and Power

My first move is to examine Michel Foucault's work on power, a conception of power that stands in sharp contrast to that of Niebuhr, offering not only what I believe to be a more compelling approach, but one that is far less abstract than Niebuhr's. For Foucault, power does not exist in some substantive sense. Foucault explains that power "is not an institution, a structure, or a certain force with which certain people are endowed." In his view, power describes "a complex strategic relation" within societies and between subjects. It cannot be possessed by one or another party. Instead, in his conception of power, power exists in and as relationship. As he puts it, "power is exercised rather than possessed."

Given this understanding, then, an analysis of power is not that of establishing some primordial base in the dynamics of the self as in Niebuhr. Rather, the analysis of power begins at the micro level, with an examination of power as a relation of force circulating systemically, "employed and exercised through a net-like organization." On my reading of Foucault, his use of the word *force* suggests the general idea of the ability to cause an effect. Thus understood, his claim that power is essentially a relation of force conveys the idea that power is a relation that has an effect.[24] As such, force should not be equated with coercion. Rather, coercion is one type of effect, but the concept of effect includes other factors of a noncoercive kind. Further, I take it that Foucault uses the metaphor of "net-like organization" to suggest the highly complex connections of discourses and practices in a given form or forms of life.

Because power is not a substance that exists, it cannot be localized in one place or another, and, since no one possesses power, it cannot be appropriated in the manner of a commodity or riches. Neither can the subject be understood as a sort of basic unit upon which power is centered or which power can overwhelm and perhaps destroy. Indeed, Foucault maintains that "individuals circulate between its threads . . . simultaneously undergoing and exercising this power." As both inert and consenting targets of power, individuals are "the vehicles of power, not its point of application."[25] He also characterizes individuals as the ingredients "of its articulation." The point here is that power is not something that various individuals "have" (and which others "lack"), but instead has more to do with the ways the

---

24. Following Foucault's conception of power, Asad describes power as "the effect of an entire network of motivated practices." Asad points out that this network "assumes a religious form" in terms of the aim or end it takes on. Asad, *GR*, 35.

25. Foucault, *P/K*, 98.

relations of power circulate and obtain *between* and *through* individuals. Thus understood, the individual is not the *possessor* of power but is the *product* of it. The individual is literally produced by power as one of power's primary *effects*. As the one whom power has individuated, the individual is simultaneously a medium and conveyor of power, so that specific gestures, discourses, and desires come to compose, to be the same as, the individual.[26]

Foucault considers the individual, as both effect and articulating element of power, to be the paradox of subjectivation, indicating that the subordination of the subject by way of the processes and conditions of power is the formative mode by which the subject develops self-consciousness, identity, and agentive capacity. His point here is that the analysis of power should not concern itself with "conscious intention or decision" or with an individual's "internal point of view." Analyses of power that focus on who "possesses" power and the nature of their intentions are misguided because such approaches ask a "labyrinthine and unanswerable question." Instead, to explore power in terms of its internal aims (if there are any) requires thorough attention to what Foucault calls "its real and effective practices." For this reason, he argues that power must be studied at the point of its "direct and immediate relationship with that which we can provisionally call its object, its target, its field of application, . . . where it installs itself and produces its real effects."[27] For Foucault, in other words, analyses of power require the identification of the practices directly involved in the functioning of mechanisms of power. Thus he eschews generalized abstractions like "class" or "nation" in order to focus on "the cells and most basic units of society."[28] I interpret him to mean here the ways of thinking and acting, the discourses and practices, of a form of life.

An important aspect of Foucault's concept of power is the method he employs to understand it. Specifically, Foucault does not attempt to arrive at conclusions about power by considering formations of power in terms of a pyramid with an apex from which one may begin a study, subsequently proceeding by working down to the base of that power. Neither does he analyze power using a center-to-periphery model in which those at the center have power and thereby control those at the periphery. Rather, Foucault provides an *ascending* analysis of power, which begins at the micro

---

26. Ibid.

27. Ibid., 97.

28. Ibid., 100f. As Asad says, power is "the effect of an entire network of practices." See *GR*, 35.

level with what he calls the "infinitesimal mechanisms" of power, each with a history of its own, with its particular trajectory, techniques, and tactics.[29] The task of analysis is to discover how these "mechanisms of power" were and are "invested, colonized, utilized, involuted, transformed, displaced, extended, etc., by ever more general mechanisms and by forms of global domination."[30] As he famously characterized it, the purpose of analysis is "to locate power at the extreme points of its exercise."[31] It is this focus on the concrete discourses and practices of power at a micro level that represents one of Foucault's major contributions to its study.

Importantly, Foucault maintains that the strategic relations of power that he describes are not univocal. That is, power is not exercised simply as an obligation or a prohibition on those who "do not have it." Instead, power invests individuals and is transmitted *by* them and *through* them; moreover, it exerts pressure on them, just as they themselves, in their struggle against it, resist the grip it has on them. The points of confrontation in these relations of power and in the centers of instability generated thereby are without number. This means that relations of power go right down into the depths of society, so that relations of power are not localized in either the relations between the state and its citizens or in the relations between classes. Furthermore, relations of power do not merely reproduce, at the level of individuals, bodies, gestures, and behavior, the general form of the law or government.[32]

Finally, Foucault was well aware that the risks of conflict and struggle and the potential for even brief reversals of power permeate these relations. Yet, even if there is an overturning of these powers at this micro level, this overturning is not an "all or nothing" event. For example, even when power shifts in a dramatic way—as in a political coup d'état or the eradication of an institution—and sweeping changes occur, none of these changes per se constitutes an overthrow of power, as if there formerly was power and suddenly power is gone. Rather, such changes indicate a shift in power relations. But the precise nature of a power shift, whether a takeover, an innovation, or the destruction of an institution, depends on the impact of this

---

29. By techniques or technologies Foucault means the "joinings of knowledge and power" that address the body "as an object to be manipulated and controlled." Rabinow, "Introduction," in *FR*, 17. See also the helpful discussion by Gordon, "Afterword," in *P/K*, 237–38.

30. Ibid., 99.

31. Ibid., 97.

32. Ibid.

shift on the entire network of relations in which it is enmeshed.³³ That is, power has not been either eliminated or destroyed as much as its relations have been rearranged.

POWER/TRUTH

Obviously, in a complex society the relations of power are manifold, such that they "permeate, characterize and constitute the social body." At the same time, relations of power do not come from nowhere. Foucault argues that relations of power always require establishment, consolidation, and implementation through "the production, accumulation, circulation and functioning of a discourse." An individual cannot use power apart from the production of truth in this sense.³⁴ Power and truth are thus co-constituted and thoroughly interdependent for Foucault. While he believes this relationship between truth and power characterizes any society, Foucault maintains that this relationship "is organized in a highly specific fashion" in each particular society. For this reason, he holds, "we are forced to produce the truth of power that our society demands," the kind of power it requires in order to operate.³⁵ In describing the compulsion to "produce the truth of power that our society demands," Foucault explains:

> In the last analysis, we must produce truth as we must produce wealth, indeed we must produce truth in order to produce wealth in the first place. . . . It is truth that makes the laws, that produces the true discourse which, at least partially, decides, transmits and itself extends upon the effects of power. In the end, we are judged, condemned, classified, determined in our undertakings, destined to a certain mode of living or dying, as a function of the true discourses which are the bearers of the specific effects of power.³⁶

As Foucault uses the word, *truth* is the framing of what can be said and done in a form of life. By truth Foucault does not mean, for example, some accurate correspondence of a discourse with the actual state of affairs in some final or ultimate sense. Truth is a relationship of intelligibility between discourses and practices and a form of life. It is a range of practices that shape thinking and acting in a specific form of life. As we are formed,

33. Ibid.
34. *P/K*, 93.
35. Ibid.
36. Ibid., 93f.

we are subjected to the production of truth—what can be said and done—through the effects of power.

MACRO POWER

The ascending analysis of power Foucault proposes raises questions about macro-level power, especially at the level of the state and the economy. Some criticize Foucault by claiming that he does not have an adequate understanding of larger patterns of power.[37] Yet, Foucault is quite explicit that he does not intend to minimize state power as unimportant or ineffective. His concern, rather, is the way that conventional understandings of state power treat the state itself as the primary instrument and locus of power, thereby failing to see many of the more subtle and discrete mechanisms and effects of power that are not directly dictated, controlled, or executed by the state apparatus, even though they function to uphold the state "more effectively" than the institutions that constitute it, thereby magnifying and increasing its effectiveness.[38] Foucault maintains that a state "is more than just a government." His point is that while the state certainly has political-military forces, political parties, technicians, specialists, and other functionaries operating within its purview, to identify the state apparatus as the sole or even primary seat of power would be a mistake. Foucault recognized that the material exercise of power moves through a great many "finer channels" and is far more mixed in its workings.[39]

On my reading of Foucault, his approach does not neglect macro questions. It is rather the case that he begins his analysis at a very concrete, material level that focuses on the practices, discourses, and technologies of particular relations of power. He wants to avoid abstractions like "the state" or "sovereignty" or "the juridical" that cover over precisely what it is that most needs careful unpacking and analysis. I believe that Foucault's treatment of power suggests that at the macro level, the focus needs to be on the practices of large groups of people and on the discourses operative there—that is, on the technologies in use and the apparatuses at work. He suggests larger patterns of a great range of techniques and practices, which involve discipline, surveillance, and administration in the formation of populations of people. I think here, too, of large-scale practices such as

37. Best and Kellner, *Postmodern Theory*, 71–72.
38. *P/K*, 72–73.
39. Ibid., 59f.

Niebuhr's Concept of Power

public civic spectacles whose object of veneration is the nation-state—for example, recitations of the Pledge of Allegiance in a host of venues, including some of very large scale, or of the mixture of patriotism and other arenas of devotion in large gatherings such as worship, baseball games, political rallies, and so forth.

Foucault insists that when analyzing macro-level displays of power, the focus must be upon their mechanisms, their effects and their relations. His point is not that there ought not to be concrete, material examinations of the practices of macro power, but that macro-level structures such as the economy, the state, or some other large-scale abstraction cannot be fully understood without careful attention to the many effects at work in these and that full accounting of these effects will take one far afield from the actual apparatus itself. His point, I daresay, is that if one abstractly theorizes the derivation of power from the economy or government or their interrelation, any number of interpretations are quite possible—limitless, in human terms—and also quite ungrounded materially if theorized apart from discourses, technologies, and practices.

FOUCAULT VERSUS NIEBUHR

Even my short summary of Foucault's conception of power indicates sharp contrasts with how Niebuhr understands power. Niebuhr works from a primordial, existentialist view of the self, whereas Foucault understands the subject as formed from power relations, with agency emerging as an effect of these dynamics. Niebuhr sees power as participating in a Christian view of creation and therefore as good, even if perennially subject to abuse, misuse, and corruption. Foucault sees power not only in terms of its coercive capacities but in terms of its productive and creative ones as well, and one of his priorities is to push back against attempts to cast power in negative and repressive terms alone, or even primarily.

In terms of the source of power, Niebuhr understands it as emerging from the vitalities of spirit and nature in the self and as virtually synonymous with energy. For Foucault, while the energies of the body are certainly involved, power is a relation of force or effect rather than a substance; and he characterizes it as a relation that is both complex and strategic. Niebuhr understands the will to power as growing out of the arrogance of an anxious freedom, or pride. For Foucault, power is not a product of the wills and interests of subjects, but rather operates through discourse, practices, and technologies. The upshot of this understanding of how power operates is that a subject is not *prior* to the power that constitutes it but is, indeed, the *effect* of that power. In Foucault's view, a subject's agency is not inherent to or located within it, but can only arise in the complexity of those forces that make that subject possible. Therefore, contra Niebuhr, it is not the vitalities of the self that precede power, in Foucault's view, but power drawing on and forming the energies of the body that constitute the subject.

Niebuhr, as we have seen, certainly understands power in terms of a massive range of unlimited configurations in human terms. While the dynamics of the self operate in all constructions of power, social power rests upon a number of factors, including differentiations of social function and expressions of social organization and cohesion; a field of vitality elaborated in consensual and conflictive forms; the work of a conscious political effort to moderate conflict and to conjure instruments for more encompassing mutualities of social existence; the harmony of communities; and the relative stability, but also the uncertainties, of the harmonies of human vitality.

As I read this list of the sources of social power, I am struck by their abstractness when considered from a Foucauldian perspective. How much more concrete and materially based it would be were Niebuhr to elucidate major discourses, practices, and technologies that characterize each of the factors he names! Take a matter like "differentiations of social function." Suppose one were to take the differentiations that occurred between politics, economics, religious institutions, and other major dimensions of more traditional societies in the rise of the modern period, and probe into the discourses and actual practices that constituted the field of each of these social relations. In Foucauldian terms, I am suggesting an elaboration and articulation of the concrete, actual relations that create the differentiations Niebuhr observed. Or, take Niebuhr's notion of social life as comprised of many forms that involve both mutual support and conflict—for instance, practices of support and conflict in farming communities or urban neighborhoods. It seems to me that Niebuhr's language obscures the actual, specific practices of which these forms are made. I contend that it is these practices that require examination if we are to adequately describe the character of "the mutualities" or the "conflict."

Or, take the relationship that Niebuhr sees between law and the vitalities of life. It is not enough to argue that the harmony of communities is not to be found simply in the authority of law. This may well be the case, but it tells us nothing about what "the harmony of communities" *does* consist of. Rather, again, careful attention must be given to the material discourses, practices, and technologies at work producing specific instances of social harmony. I think, too, of the important role that practices, discourses, and technologies play in Niebuhr's discussions of "majesty" and "prestige" as these relate to the function of government. What do majesty and prestige look like in terms of the concrete practices and discourses that create, maintain, and sustain them? Absent the ability to articulate their micro practices, these concepts are but vague abstractions with no real grounding in *actual* social and political life.

It would be easy to go on with these kinds of examples of the specificity that Niebuhr lacks. Suffice it to say that Niebuhr's development of the notion of power suffers from this very lack of concrete materiality—this, in spite of his quite evident concern to be "empirical." Were it not for Niebuhr's extraordinary capacity to capture the imagination of his audiences with compelling generalizations that brook no exceptions, I suspect that the lack of empirical justification would be stunningly clear. Indeed, a closer examination of Niebuhr's existential self to determine the actual practices of introspection at work in people's subjective experience would reveal a great range of reflexive states. I am confident that these would not line up with Niebuhr's dualisms of transcendence and finitude or arrogance and sloth. In saying this, it is not my intent to make the subject more ideal. One consequence would be to make sin, for example, far more complex than Niebuhr's limited view provides, as O'Donovan indicates. Furthermore, I wonder if Niebuhr's trademark neglect of definitions and his willingness to use words like *self-interest* and *power* in so many different ways is not a result of that great mind knowing—or, if not that, intuiting—a complexity that requires a type of grounding that his level of conceptualization and thought does not provide. I shall return to these issues in chapter 4 in order to provide an example that works with discourses, practices, and technologies in a power conflict in order to call into question in the sharpest terms Niebuhr's view of the self, of interest, and of power.

To summarize my critique of Niebuhr's concept of power so far, I argue first for a position like that of Foucault, who offers "an ascending analysis" of power that focuses on "real and effective practices." In this understanding, power is "exercised rather than possessed." Central to Foucault's understanding of power is domination, which more typically takes place through the range of discourses, practices, and technologies that produce normalcy.

Such an understanding of power requires the production of truth, with the latter understood as what can be said and done in a form or forms of life. Even with his focus on micro power, Foucault's focus on discourse and practices can readily address macro issues with this kind of focus. The value of Foucault's analysis resides in its capacity to avoid abstraction by means of its capacity to focus on both micro and macro power. It is at this point that we have found Niebuhr's work to be far too abstract and offer Foucault as an important corrective.

With this critique in place we are now in a position to examine the key role that the concept of the balance of power plays in Niebuhr's social thought.

4

The Balance of Power in Niebuhr's Social Thought

CENTRAL TO NIEBUHR'S SOCIAL thought and his understanding of power is the notion of balance, or equilibrium, of power. This concept shapes his understanding of justice, qualifies the way that he sees Christian love operating in the world, and plays a key role in his understanding of history. Niebuhr's social thought cannot be understood apart from his concept of the balance of power. It is here we can see the impact of his understanding of human nature and of the role of self-interest on the crucial issue of power, and the necessity of working for a basic distribution of power in the complexities, ambiguities, and vicissitudes of social life. In this section, I shall first outline his basic view of the balance of power and, then, drawing on Michael Sheehan's work, turn to sketching a short history of the variety of uses of this concept in the West. Finally, I will end with a critique of the overly abstract and insufficiently historical way in which Niebuhr conceived of this dynamic of power.

As we have seen, Niebuhr understands power to be closely bound up with the great range of human vitalities—so closely bound up with them, as Stone suggests, that power in Niebuhr's thought can be conceived as basically human energy and the structures and forms that it takes. In this vein, Niebuhr writes, "All communities are more or less stable or precarious harmonies of human vital capacities. They are governed by power."[1] In this discussion of the function of power in communities, Niebuhr examines power in two modes: first, in terms of the relationship of government (i.e.,

1. *NDM*2, 257. See his even stronger language on this point in *SNE*, 149, 181.

the organization of power in the state), and, second, in the wider community (i.e., the balance of power). Crucially, he notes that power cannot be reduced simply to coercion, or the arrangements of government. Rather, government is but one of two distinct dimensions of social power. Naming government as "the central organizing principle of power," he refers to the other dimension of social power as "the equilibrium of power," or "the balance of vitalities and forces in any given situation." Niebuhr sees both of these dimensions as fundamentally constitutive elements of communal life. Social life, in other words, emerges and exists on the basis of government *and* the social equilibrium of power among groups in the wider community. Lacking one or the other, social life itself will cease to exist as such, and hence there is no improvement, morally or socially, that frees society from the determinative impact of these two factors.[2]

Both governmental power and the balance of power are the dynamic bedrock at the foundation of social life, yet Niebuhr understands government, or at least what he calls "the principle of government," as representing "a higher plane of moral sanction and social necessity" than the second dimension, the balance of power. Government has the role of organizing the range of social vitalities, and without this role, he believes these vitalities would simply degenerate into anarchy. Furthermore, Niebuhr understands government as "a more conscious effort to arrive at justice" than the dynamics of the balance of power that he saw as representing a more intuitive and thereby less direct set of social processes. On his view, government belongs to the realm of the *historical*, while these vitalities belong to the realm of the *natural*.[3]

The fact that Niebuhr placed government in the realm of conscious and distinctly human history by no means implies that government is thereby exempt from abuse. Niebuhr identifies two abuses to which government is prone and that make for moral ambiguity. The first of these abuses occurs when one or more groups in the community achieve domination through government, so that the government is used to advance their own power, interest, and gain. The other abuse occurs when government itself is not subject to sufficient checks and balances or restraints and, as a result, takes on imperious impulses of its own in the name of order. In such cases, a government identifies the particular order it promotes as the equivalent

---

2. *NDM*1, 257–58.
3. Ibid., 266.

of the principle of order itself, thereby falling into what Niebuhr considers "idolatry and pretension."[4]

A full understanding of the idolatry and pretension Niebuhr has in mind requires recognition of how governments derive the power they hold. For Niebuhr, governmental power has two sources, one of which is what he calls "the pretension of majesty" and the other what he calls "reality." His point in drawing this distinction is that no government or ruler can govern with the tools of coercion alone, and he sees quite clearly that the authority of government does not rely only on "'rational' consent." Something like "uncoerced submission" is utterly indispensable for effective political rule. According to Niebuhr, such uncoerced submission requires an "explicitly or implicitly, religious reverence for 'majesty.'"[5] Further, he held that the majesty of government requires "legitimate pretensions of majesty and sanctity." Niebuhr's notion of majesty as pretension refers to an inclination of governments to conceal and disguise the conditional and limited "cast of their dominion and to assert unconditional legitimation for it."[6] This level of legitimacy occurs only when government both "embodies and expresses" a community-encompassing authority and power so as to hold all its members in allegiance. It is majesty in this sense that can stand against the dangers of anarchy through the establishment of a form of order and justice.

Obviously, pretensions of majesty can lead to great abuse and can suppress quite appropriate resistance to government. How to address this issue is a major political problem. Niebuhr contends that the highest achievement of democratic societies is how they are able to build resistance to government within the structure of government itself. This achievement means that there is a constitutional basis for citizens to counter unjust intrusions of government without thereby generating anarchy. Where criticism is understood as intrinsic to good government, it can function as a tool of, and not a menace to, political rule. At the same time, Niebuhr identifies an emergent tension in modern societies between economic and political power whereby economic power tends to concentrate and to create conditions of injustice, while political power tends to become increasingly dispersed. As a result, political power operates to counter the injustices caused by concentrations of economic power. He thus believes that the struggle

---

4. *NDM*2, 267.
5. Ibid.
6. Ibid., 268. On "majesty" see also *SNE*, 8, 34f.

between these two forms of power is crucial to understanding modern democratic capitalist societies.

Economic oligarchies attempt to influence political power to serve their designs, an effort never fully attained. Countering concentrations of power in the economic order is what Niebuhr calls "the political power of the common man [sic]." This power he sees as holding the potential to serve political and economic justice, even though Niebuhr readily admits that political power has not been fully successful at routing "flagrant forms of economic injustice."[7]

It is important to remember here that for Niebuhr social power is composed of an immense variety of different forms, alliances, coalitions, and associations. It includes as well a plenitude of factors, everything from a persuasive rationality to coercive force. Further, differentiations of social functions generate not only power but also different kinds of power, and include, of course, economic and political power.[8] The picture here is one of an immense, diverse, historically and socially contingent range of spiritual and natural vitalities and forms that constitute power in the complicated relationships of human life. Clearly, Niebuhr's concept of power is immense in scope. In fact, its scope is so wide-ranging that I venture to say that anything that has energy is power on Niebuhr's view.

If, in Niebuhr's view, anything that has energy is power, this means that a balance of power is necessarily very complex in any given situation, let alone across time. Moreover, I do not get any sense that Niebuhr thinks of this equilibrium of power as static. While it may be relatively stable for a given time, the balance of power seems always for Niebuhr to refer to a dynamic equilibrium. To elaborate, a balance of power is a complex dynamic made up of social restraints that he says are "armed" with resources. Within this dynamic, disputes between opposing or disagreeing parties can be composed and articulated by appeals to reason and conscience. In situations of conflict, any available resource can be brought to bear by any party. Even so, he says that conflict is usually "subdued by and composed by superior force and authority." Thus the threat of force (for instance, by government or a party to a conflict) is significant in all communal relations. Here we see that the dynamic and relational character of the balance of power is so tenuous that in the context of a conflict, the explicit disavowal by a party to use a resource under its control is an act that is actually

---

7. *NDM*2, 261–62.
8. Ibid.

capable of upsetting the equilibrium of social forces that existed prior to that disavowal. Consequently, the advantage in the conflict may well fall to another party that *is* prepared to use any resource at its disposal.[9]

So the balance of power, the second dimension of social power, is complicated not only in terms of the competition and conflicts between various parties in a community, but also by the fact that each of these parties in itself is internally constituted of equilibria of power.[10] The multiple layers of a balance of power can be seen in a struggle between labor and manufacturing companies in a community's balance of power. To focus exclusively on the power dynamics between the two primary parties in the struggle is a misguided strategy. It is also necessary to look at the balance of power *within* the companies and *within* labor itself. The result, of course, is that these equilibria increase in complexity and in layerings when conceived in this way. Niebuhr also discusses power equilibria within family life and other such interpersonal relationships. The balance of power is worked out in innumerable sites since, in his view, "all social life represents a field of vitality, elaborated in many forms, which are related to each other in terms of both mutual support and of potential conflict."[11] In summary, power is ubiquitous in social life. The complexities of its relationships both at the level of the entire community and at the level of interpersonal relations are innumerable and multilayered.

THE INTERNATIONAL BALANCE OF POWER

When Niebuhr moves from an examination of a community or a nation-state to the international arena, at least two things are different. First, government plays a different role. There is no world government, which means that without some transcending form of authority, the relationships of the nation-states are always threatened by anarchy. To the extent that there is relative stability and peace among the world's nations, it is due to a balance of power or, more typically, to some circumstance in which the more powerful nations are held in check by one another through their alliances, thereby functioning as countervailing powers among themselves. Given

---

9. Ibid., 259–60.
10. Ibid., 262.
11. Ibid., 265, see 248.

the absence of a global government, the international balance of power becomes the central category in Niebuhr's political analysis.[12]

The second shift as Niebuhr moves from communal and national analyses to an international one is the lack of unity and cohesion among the nation-states. In *The Structure of Nations and Empires* Niebuhr argues that the pluralistic makeup of Western communities is radically different from the dynamics that characterize the international arena. The power arrangements of a pluralistic society in which there are "many centers of power and of ideological prestige in the culture" are not the result of happenstance or accident. Rather, Niebuhr points out that without a range of resources—"educational, moral, and spiritual"—there would not have been the kind of "tolerance" that a pluralistic community requires as a basic condition of possibility. In addition, the stability of a pluralistic society also would not be possible without the same kinds of resources. He further argues that pluralistic societies require certain "basic affinities" on which the underlying social unity can rest, such as the affinity in the United States between the three forms of biblical faith—Catholicism, Protestantism, and Judaism—along with a "secular humanism" that does not seriously challenge and at times even reinforces basic views of this "common faith." This underlying unity provides a base that can sustain certain differences. Niebuhr argues that this unity is also accompanied by a level of economic prosperity that was sufficient to offset the kind of social conflict that otherwise might have developed between socioeconomic classes.[13]

Niebuhr points out that this kind of unity and cohesion is largely confined to nation-states and tends to disappear in international affairs. While the emerging global community is clearly pluralistic in culture, economics, and politics, this global plurality lacks the unity and cohesion characteristic of a nation-state.[14]

---

12. *NDM*2, 284–86.

13. *SNE*, 293–94. Niebuhr does warn against any self-congratulation by those in the "open societies" of the West, saying, "The virtues and the stabilities of Western pluralistic cultures and communities are thus a bequest of historical 'providence,'" well beyond the designs of any of the actors in that history. See also *SDH*, 217.

14. *SNE*, 294. In the context of this discussion he names explicitly "the conflict of power" between Russia and the United States.

BIPOLAR POWER AND THE BALANCE OF TERROR

During the late 1930s and the early 1940s Niebuhr's focus on the balance of power took as its primary point of departure the threat of the rising Nazi and fascist forces in Europe and the imperial activity of the Japanese. While he was certainly attentive to Russia and highly critical of the Marxist-Leninist communism there, he was most interested in how power was distributed immediately prior to and during World War II. During the war years he maintained that new responsibilities would be thrust upon the United States in the emerging world order. He was staunchly against isolationism, on the one hand, and imperialism, on the other (although he predicted that the new responsibilities that the United States would take on in the postwar world order would bring charges of the latter). At the same time, while he recognized a new role for his country, he cautioned against the dangers of arrogance and the temptations of a powerful nation to be blind to the finitude of its own power.[15]

In the late 1940s and 1950s, however, Niebuhr's attention turns from the immediate implications of World War II to its aftermath, and specifically to the new distribution of power between the United States and the USSR—a distribution that he describes as bipolar. He characterizes the modern world—by which he meant the postwar political situation that was quickly setting up for the Cold War—as "divided by two opposing alliances of nations," the "two imperialisms today." With this structure composed of the two competing alliances, Niebuhr observes that each alliance was subordinate to "the hegemony of a nation"—that is, to Russia, on the one hand, and to the United States, on the other—that held the economic and military strength to set the policy for their respective alliances. He describes the leadership of Russia as "more obviously ideological" than that of the United States. As "the 'fatherland' of communism," Russia was essentially required to provide support for any country that decided to embrace communism—for instance, the governments of Poland, Hungary, and East Germany. In contrast, Niebuhr saw the hegemony of the United States as "not as consistently ideological" and as leading an alliance made up of both Western democracies and many other Eastern and Western noncommunist states, including, notably, Britain, France, and West Germany. Of course, in reality, few of the United States' allies actually saw the United States as the perfect model of "the democratic creed." More typically, the United States' allies

---

15. Stone, *RNPP*, 180.

simply regarded it as the most powerful country relative to those in their orbit.[16] Indeed, Niebuhr saw the power that secured U.S. authority both nationally and internationally as a "curious mixture of force and prestige." Though he believed that prestige is more significant than force in national life, he held that in international relations force takes on significantly more gravity.[17] Hence, both the United States and the Soviet Union dominated their respective alliances by virtue of their economic and military strength and their prestige and force in a bipolar balance of power.

Following World War II, the bipolar balance of power between Russia and the United States took on even more serious proportions as the Soviets developed nuclear weaponry to counter that of the United States. Stone characterizes Niebuhr's Cold War view of the two nations as "essentially of two nuclear-armed scorpions locked in a small bottle."[18] Moreover, Niebuhr believed that the two nations were basically equal in their capacities to devastate and destroy each other. With the development of inventive guided missiles to launch attacks, the terror of this equilibrium changed the entire military makeup of each country and its alliances to such an extent that a "calculated policy" to enter war with the other was unthinkable. A surprise attack would bring such destruction even on the aggressor that distinctions between victory and defeat would be meaningless. Further, disarmament seemed highly improbable, and the possibility of a war brought on by "miscalculation or misadventure," although not likely, suggested to Niebuhr that the world might continue to exist in this balance of terror for some time. Should it be the case that both the Soviets and the Americans had the "wisdom and good fortune" to avoid nuclear catastrophe, Niebuhr saw each

---

16. *SNE*, 10.

17. Niebuhr clarifies that he has "substituted" the "weaker concept of 'prestige'" for that of "majesty" in discussing domestic and international relations together. The more traditional word *majesty*, which describes national authority in previous governments, is too strong to describe the contemporary situation in both foreign and domestic relations. Further, he assumes that power and authority—which derive from the two sources of prestige or majesty—are synonymous in characterizing "the capacity of a government or state to gain obedience or compliance." By "prestige" or "majesty" he means "all the forces of tradition and history which induce obedience and compliance," and by "force" "the capacity to coerce." While the use of coercion is "always minimal in a well-established state, in comparison with 'prestige' or 'majesty,'" it may serve as "the source of authority" at the rise of a state or following a revolution. Coercion exacts obedience "until the authority of government has been established, when it may win uncoerced consent by its prestige." Ibid, 8.

18. Stone, *Christian Realism and Peacemaking*, 38.

continuing to engage the other in "the inevitable rivalries of power, which are possible and indeed unavoidable, even in what is known as 'peaceful coexistence.'"[19]

In summary, power, on Niebuhr's view, is morally neutral, with its ethical status dependent upon its arrangements, its impulses, and its use. It expresses the vitality of both human spirit and nature. Power is, moreover, a necessary expression of the organization and cohesion of society. Characterized by an endless variety and boundless types, ranges, and configurations, power cannot be reduced to coercion, but is governed to a greater degree by no less dangerous spiritual aspects. It derives as well from differentiations of social function, and these vary across societies and throughout history. For example, economic power is not more basic, with other forms of power deriving from it, but it has become a dominant form of power in the modern world.

The desire to possess power can be a direct form and an indirect instrument of pride among the strong and the weak, and ostensibly those in between. Pride of power resides also in the attempt to dominate nature out of greed or in response to the threat that nature represents to human life. If the will to live can be a search for authentic life, the will to power can seek an inordinate human significance against the threatening indifference of nature and history, exacerbating a more natural will to survive and thereby conflicting with the wills of others and heightening aggression and hostility.

In all human communities government comprises one form of social power, the other form being the balance of power or the balance of vitalities and forces of that government's community, with the second of these constituting an immense, diverse, historically and socially contingent range of expressions across societies and history. Abuses of government and of imbalances of power grip the human venture, thus begetting the misery, exploitation, and domination of human wrongdoing and injustice. As such, a balance or equilibrium of power is a necessary, although insufficient, basis for a rough approximation of justice in human communities and for human flourishing.

Without world government international relations are ever under the threat of anarchy, and here the balance of power becomes central. Virtues, resources, affinities, common faith, and economic circumstances vary among the nations, and unity and cohesion among the nation-states are largely limited to the domestic scene and tend to vanish in the struggle of

---

19. *SNE*, 10f.

international competition. Furthermore, in the days of Niebuhr's mature life and thought, the world was characterized by a bipolar balance of power and a nuclear-based balance of terror between the two empires of the USSR and the United States, a situation that he foresaw continuing for some time.

Obviously, much more could be said about Niebuhr's concept of the balance of power, but this is perhaps sufficient to name some of his central claims and to move next to a critique of his point of view.

CRITIQUE OF NIEBUHR'S VIEW OF THE BALANCE OF POWER

Foucault's concept of power and his focus on the discourse, practices, and technologies of power offer a far more concrete approach to the concept of power than does Niebuhr. The implications of this are many, and none is more important than that regarding Niebuhr's concept of the balance of power, a key concept in his social thought. In this critique of Niebuhr's concept of the balance of power I argue that Niebuhr is insufficiently alert to the historicity of the concept itself, that the concept lacks clarity and exactitude in its uses in the West in the last five hundred years, and that abstract uses of the notion work against any empirical grounding of it in national and international political affairs. Further, new circumstances now call for serious modifications of the concept and its use. Basic to my argument is that the balance of power concept requires close attention to the discourses, practices, and technologies operative in those situations or arenas where it is used as a descriptive and a prescriptive concept. Otherwise, it remains a high abstraction and of highly ambiguous use. I begin this critique by examining the history of the concept.

In his study of the balance of power, political theorist Michael Sheehan observes that contemporary notions of the balance of power emerged only relatively recently, roughly at the end of the European Renaissance. The key component of this thinking was the readiness of less powerful states in the European system to enter into alliances with other states in order to fend off attempts by still other states, whether actual or potential, to encroach on their territory or interests.

Sheehan describes two basic models through which the balance of power was understood. The first was a Hobbesian notion, according to which the balance of power concept was used as a means to sustain nation-state independence within the European system by erecting a triggering mechanism to initiate alliances with some states against the "hegemonial aspirations" of others. The second used the concept of the balance of power in a Grotian framework, according to which the balance of power was viewed as a harmonizing pattern for upholding international relationships, a scheme that arose from the Treaty of Westphalia in 1648. This framework of the balance of power was invoked as the model that nations and their representatives were to follow to sustain independence and order. If, in the former, the balance of power is a mechanism for initiating the formation of alliances against power grabs by others, then in the latter it is a framework by which international relations not only are understood but after which they are modeled.[20]

It should also be noted here that the scientific revolution in the seventeenth and eighteenth centuries provided "a wealth of metaphors and a fascination for mechanics and balance."[21] Newton offered "a new unifying conception of the universe," and this "reconciling and harmonizing function" played into the "mechanical" metaphor, thus enhancing "the balance of power theory" during this time. Sheehan states, "Subsequent generations would relate these ideas to the balance of power conception popularized by the Newtonian revolution in science."[22] Thus the use of the "balance" metaphor comes from Newton and his scientific worldview.

The eighteenth century was "the Golden Age of the balance of power in theory and practice," and the concept received ongoing attention in European diplomacy.[23] Wars occurred, but they were limited and not total. Those wars, moreover, pursued a politics to limit the ambitions of other states or to sustain the status quo. Sheehan is clear that the concept of the balance of power did not, however, have "a concrete and unambiguous meaning," that certain ambiguities in the balance of power concept were not fully explored or clearly understood. He points especially to the more "minor or local balances" deemed important to the larger balance, but little attention was given to the roles these played. Neither was much consideration given to the contradiction in eighteenth-century uses of the concept. Understood as "a system," it was "self-sustaining, essentially a product of nature and morally neutral." As foreign policy, the concept took

---

20. Sheehan, *BP*, 47.
21. Ibid., 44.
22. Ibid., 46.
23. Morganthau, *Politics Among Nations*, 196, quoted in Sheehan, *BP*, 97.

on "positive moral connotations" as "something which *ought* to exist and *ought* to be worked for."[24]

The revolutionary and Napoleonic era do not "fit neatly" into the exploration of the balance of power systems in either the eighteenth or the nineteenth century, says Sheehan. They were forces of transition from one system of the balance of power to another. During this time "the classical eighteenth-century balance of power was overthrown."[25] The dominance of Napoleon across Europe left only Britain and Russia at the edges of the continent as powers able to challenge French power, but the drastic failure of Napoleon in his assault on Russia in 1812 brought French ascendancy to a halt and secured a new state of equilibrium. This experience with Napoleon brought a new appreciation for the balance of power; it became a source of idealism, a state of affairs to be positively pursued.[26] At the end of the Napoleonic era, observes Sheehan, statesmen learned that a mechanism was necessary to build an "automatic coalition" against hegemonic aggression in the new European order. As the eighteenth-century system had been a balance of power of "loose coordination," the nineteenth century would develop a much more highly organized arrangement.

Balance of power was used in a variety of ways throughout the nineteenth century, some of which were inconsistent, while others were more compatible. Some of these compatibilities in uses of the term suggested a sense of general principles that various powers thought should govern the international relations of Europe. Yet balance of power lacked standard definition or usage as a concept in the nineteenth century.[27] In his study, for example, Schroeder identifies eleven main uses of the term *balance of power* in the nineteenth century.[28] As Sheehan explains, "In fact, what the

---

24. Sheehan, *BP*, 104f. Sheehan's italics. I cannot in this space do justice to the rich descriptions Sheehan employs in his work on the complexities of international relations between Britain, France, Austria, Poland and others, but see his discussion of the eighteenth century, 97–120.

25. Sheehan, *BP*, 116.

26. Ibid., 119. Sheehan is quoting here Gulick, *Europe's Classical Balance of Power*, 129.

27. Sheehan, *BP*, 104f.

28. The eleven uses are as follows:
   1. An even or balanced distribution of power.
   2. Any existing distribution of power.
   3. Any existing general situation or status quo, with no particular regard to power relations.

nineteenth century revealed was that the balance of power concept was not a fixed reality, but an approach subject to the effects of the revolution of thought and indeed of broader cultural developments."[29] Thus, while balance of power was not "a meaningless mantra" in the nineteenth century, its particular use in any setting requires careful delineation—and even when carefully described provides only a partial account of action in the political arena.[30]

In his discussion of the balance of power in the twentieth century Sheehan writes of three competing perspectives: the concepts of the correlation of forces, of collective security, and of balancing and bandwagoning. With regard to the first, the coming of communist states in the twentieth century brought another way of thinking about the balance of power, that is, the correlation of forces. If the traditional balance of power concept emphasized states and their allies, realist assumptions about national interests, about power checking power, and about seeking stability for the sake of

---

4. The European system or order, the general framework of European politics.
5. Some indeterminate meaning involving some combination of the above.
6. As a verb to play the role of balancer, which can mean:
   a) oscillating between two sides
   b) being an arbiter between two sides, each of which roles may require either being within the balance or standing outside of it.
7. Stability, peace, and repose.
8. A shifting condition in international affairs, tending toward resolution by conflict.
9. The rule of law and guaranteed rights.
10. The general struggle for power, influence, and advantage—power politics according to the rule of raison d'etat.
11. Hegemony.

Schroeder, "Nineteenth-Century System," 137, quoted in Sheehan, *BP*, 141.

29. Sheehan, *BP*, 141f. In his discussion of the nineteenth century Sheehan draws three conclusions. First, the balance of power must not be seen as "the only organizing principle in international relations." Second, even when it has been generally "the recommended or approved" standard, it has not determined the basic foreign policy approach of all states. Third, in those cases where the balance of power is the goal openly espoused by statesmen and diplomats, it must be remembered that the concept takes on "many different meanings."

30. Ibid., 146–52. These are but a few of the differences that Sheehan discusses, but perhaps enough to see the difference between these competing concepts. With the collapse of communism in the Soviet Union and its satellites, the concept of correlation of forces "did not become the new paradigm for equilibrist thinking." But, claims Sheehan, some of its insights can be integrated into a larger concept of the balance of power.

97

security, then the correlation of forces concept took as its primary point of departure the difference between capitalism and communism. It attended to international movements, stressed domestic forces, class antagonism and other non-state agents, and emphasized the telos of history in the direction of progressive change.[31]

The second perspective competing with the balance of power concept during the twentieth century was that of collective security. Often seen as the antithesis of balance of power politics, this concept emerged after the end of World War I when many, including U.S. President Woodrow Wilson, argued that the balance of power concept had failed. Wilson believed the war had been a catastrophic failure and must not be repeated. Collective security was thus a way to avoid future wars, and Wilson claimed that the postwar world needed "not a balance of power, but a community of power; not organized rivalries, but an organized, common peace."[32]

The third competing perspective with the balance of power is bandwagoning and related strategies. Bandwagoning refers to situations in which a weaker power joins a stronger, threatening power for the sake of its own security. Hiding, or attempting to have nothing to do with active engagement in an international crisis with any of the national participants, is a related strategy. Also related is transcending, or attempts to rise above an anarchic international situation and to move past "the normal limits of conflictual politics by striving for an international consensus or formal agreement on norms, rules and procedures to solve the problem, end the

---

31. Ibid.

32. Quoted in Sheehan, *BP,* 152. While the collective security perspective did not maintain its Wilsonian character, and made a contribution to balance of power thinking, says Sheehan, collective security and balance of power are not "polar opposites." They share similarities, such as the attempt to manage power in international relations, a confidence in the general usefulness of deterrence, a common focus on systemic security, the conviction that one state's security is bound up with that of others, and that both concepts are devised to deal with basically the same kind of world.

But there are also real differences. Balance of power approaches seek "competitive alliance"; collective security reaches for "universal alliance." While both approaches seek to restrain and direct power, the balance of power procedure "manipulates rivalry" while collective security attempts to bring interests into harmony and to develop cooperation. In the balance of power model conflict is normative; and in collective security it is the exception. While the balance of power seeks "competitive security," collective security aims for "cooperative security." Finally, the balance of power seeks to contain not only aggression but hegemonic moves as well. It focuses more on the distribution of power and provides more latitude for individual states. Collective security offers a greater place for normative rules and understands all war and aggression as "intrinsically evil."

threat, and prevent its recurrence."³³ Finally, buckpassing is a strategy typically used in a multipolar balance of power where a weaker state attempts to pass responsibility on to other nations or agents.³⁴ Regarding all of these, Sheehan concludes that adopting policies to promote the creation of balance of power policies cannot be taken as a strategy that a state will automatically pursue as the self-evident, most rational course.

Sheehan observes that scholars working in international relations have more typically used "broad patterns of behavior" to sustain arguments for balance of power views. What is needed, he asserts, is "more detailed research." More thoroughly historical studies that focus on particular periods of history may very well disclose that balance of power theory has played a greater role in providing "an ideological function in justifying policy" than that of "a prescriptive purpose in mandating it." Such studies may well require more exact clarity about what diplomats and policymakers are thinking when they speak of the "balance of power or international equilibrium."³⁵

Even with this cursory overview of Sheehan's work, we gain insight into the historicity of the concept, its lack of a concrete and unambiguous meaning, its varied uses, the competition of other perspectives, its inexact use in covering broad patterns of behavior, its ideological functions, and the need for more careful examination of the details of its use in specific international settings. As I shall indicate in the conclusions of this chapter, these findings heavily qualify Niebuhr's work with the concept and call for a different focus in approach. But we must turn first to other issues, with the first being the balance of terror.

THE BALANCE OF TERROR

After the United States used atomic weapons against Japan in 1945, what Sheehan has termed a "Manichaean nuclear confrontation" began when the Soviet Union developed weaponry that was approximately as devastating as the weaponry of the United States. Some argued that nuclear weapons made the balance of power concept irrelevant, but Sheehan maintains that

---

33. Ibid., 164. In these first three strategies Sheehan is working with Schroeder; the quotation is from Schroeder, "Neo-Realist Theory of International Politics," 4.

34. This point is made by Barry Posen, *Sources of Military Doctrine*, 63, but the quote is Sheehan's, *BP*, 166.

35. Sheehan, *BP*, 167.

such an assessment was not entirely accurate. Although nuclear deterrence certainly affected the international system, deterrence as such was not new to the struggles among the nations. While there are certainly differences between the balance of power and the post-1945, Cold War balance of terror, the nature of foreign policy among these superpowers turned again in a more Hobbesian direction and the Grotian framework for a balance of power was abandoned as priorities shifted toward military buildup.[36]

Sheehan observes that even while the nuclear stalemate forestalled actual warfare between the United States and the Soviet Union, it also led to greater competition in the development of conventional military resources and to the strain of such costs on the national budgets and economies of these superpowers. Further, the great dangers of this nuclear stalemate brought about efforts at arms control, spurred by a growing realization that the superpowers had common interests even in spite of their major differences. Late in this era, during the Gorbachev-Shevardnadze leadership in the Kremlin, the approach to the balance of power began to shift into one "recognizably similar" to the post-1815 situation in western Europe. With the collapse of the Soviet Union, this more Grotian approach to the balance of power came once again into prominence.[37]

The end of the twentieth century brought a very different world—most notably a marked decline of the sovereign nation. Further, security can no longer be reduced to military considerations but must address burgeoning issues raised by economic and ecological threats.[38] Sheehan's book was published in 1996, so that issues of new forms of terrorism had not emerged with the significance they would take on subsequently, and especially after September 11, 2001, at least for those in the United States. Moreover, the challenges of international economic forces and of global monopoly capitalism were not as clear then as they are now. Add to this the increasing clarity of the threat presented by global warming, and the result is an illustrative but not complete list. The implications of all of these challenges for the balance of power are considerable.

Sheehan's argument is that the balance of power will continue to be an important concept in the nation-state system, but in its Grotian rather than its Hobbesian form. He explains that the Grotian form possesses much greater promise in reducing not only war but also the threat of war.

36. Ibid., 200.
37. Ibid.
38. Ibid., 202.

Sheehan believes that the Grotian alternative provides "a more mature version of 'anarchy'" and supports the strengthening of "the societal elements of the international system."[39]

For my purposes, a number of conclusions can be drawn from Sheehan's analysis of the history of the concept of balance of power. First, there can be no question that the concept is historically located, coming as it does with the rise of the system of nation-states from the late fifteenth century on. The historicity of this concept to which Sheehan so carefully attends raises questions with reference to how Niebuhr treats it. That is, while Niebuhr treats power and the balance of power with considerable complexity, I do not find him sufficiently alert to a history of the concept of the balance of power itself. This is strange, in one sense, because Niebuhr spends a good deal of his literary work reflecting on history—for example, that of the ancient world, the medieval era, the Renaissance, Romanticism, idealism, etc.—and he seems quite alert to shifts in the mid-twentieth century with regard to the balance of power when examined in the light of the Cold War–era balance of terror. Yet, in another sense, it may be an unfair criticism because the work of people like Foucault made the historical study of discourse and concepts more prominent only at the very end of and after Niebuhr's life. My purpose is not to attack Niebuhr unfairly. It is, however, to suggest that avoiding attention to the historicity of the balance of power is no longer defensible. Today, moving to more specific and historically informed perspectives on such questions is imperative. Second, Sheehan's analysis further shows the extent to which the meaning of balance of power as a concept is not fixed but varies considerably. As we have seen, Sheehan suggests that this concept is typically used in ways that he characterizes as either Hobbesian or Grotian. Though helpful in a broad sense, these characterizations are high abstractions, and to apply them to the different historical eras as he does without devolving into a label with manifold meanings requires considerable specificity. The risk here is that, as labels, "Hobbesian" and "Grotian" clarify little about what balance of power means and entails in any particular situation, and thus these characterizations are no substitute for careful analysis. Without attention to specificity, they obscure and thereby miss a host of dynamics that are crucial to the analysis of a particular situation, a point that Sheehan recognizes in his call for more careful and exact research. On my view, following Foucault, big abstractions like the balance of power require detailed examination of the

---

39. Ibid., 204f.

operative discourses, practices, and technologies at work in the international system, where that concept serves to obscure a closer descriptive and prescriptive approach.

Third, it is also quite clear that balance of power is but one of a number of forms of power relations that have been and currently are in use. International relations, in other words, do not boil down essentially or exclusively to balance of power. In terms of Niebuhr, alternative strategies such as bandwagoning, hiding, transcending, and buckpassing name different complexities of power that a too exclusive focus on the balance of power does not adequately address. These strategies make it clear that a balance of power approach is not an automatic response and cannot be assumed. As Sheehan suggests, international relations scholars have resorted to "broad patterns" to support the balance of power concept, and what is needed is "more detailed research." Because of this more general approach, in part, balance of power theory has played more of "an ideological function" in justifying policy, and far less frequently a diagnostic role that then directs a course of action.

Fourth, it also seems clear that what Sheehan terms the Hobbesian variant of the balance of power does ebb and flow in the history of the concept. Its recent appearance in the twentieth century, as we have seen, testifies to some durability of the concept, even if it must be abstractly conceived to fit more historically specific settings. At the same time, it would be a grave mistake to attempt to reduce Niebuhr's thought to a strictly Hobbesian framework. If anything, Niebuhr as a political, ethical, and theological realist is something of a blend of both the Hobbesian and Grotian views. Be that as it may, Niebuhr's elaborations of human nature, self-interest, and the will to power place the weight of his thought about the balance of power in a more Hobbesian conceptuality, and consequently his position suffers from the difficulties I have identified above in his concepts of human nature and self-interest and the abstractions of his work with the concept of power itself. Finally, as Sheehan observes, we entered a new time in the late twentieth century. The sovereignty of nation-states is no longer a given, and many issues arise that cannot be fully and adequately addressed by these political agents alone. In a discussion of nations, cultures, and empires, Niebuhr speaks explicitly to a capacity for self-destruction due to the "idolization of an ephemeral institution." He writes that these institutions tend either to "estimate their own power too highly or they regard some form of social organization, a certain equilibrium of social forces, a given class structure, or a traditional constitutional procedure as final and absolute." In other words, they fail to recognize the contingent character of all historic forms.[40] If we are at a time when the nation-state system is ending or when a major unanticipated modification of it is at work, it would be an ironic testimony to Niebuhr's sense of the contingency of all social forms should the concept of the balance of power take its place in the dustbins of history.

As I said in the introduction, Niebuhr's generalizations are like lightning bolts on a dark night in the way that they illuminate the landscape in a stunning and unforgettable manner. The problem, however, is that the illumination given by lightning and that given by full sunlight are not the same. In full daylight, the particularities and complexities of the terrain are made apparent in ways not completely disclosed by even a gigantic burst of luminosity in the dark. Niebuhr's writing conveys a sense that power is extraordinarily complex and that the balance of power takes on many forms. Yet the way he conceptualizes power and the balance of power does not *concretely* convey that complexity. His work is not able to help us with either the conceptual refinement or the specific detail required for more adequate description.

Further, Niebuhr's view of the nature of the self, of the role of self-interest, and of the determinative place of power in social life and history bolsters a confidence in their empirical intelligibility that turns out to be illusory. When compared with Mahmood's careful attention to the particularity of her subjects (chapter 1), with Hirschmann's detailed historical account of the concept of interest (chapter 2), and with Sheehan's study of the history of the concept of the balance of power in this chapter, Niebuhr's work seems so wide-sweeping and abstract that its descriptive power is compromised; it seems to beg for a more adequate empirical grounding. Though his generalizations often seem profound and compelling, when examined in light of the history of discourse or explored for concrete practices at the micro and macro levels of material life, his work is not adequate. It begs for conceptual refinement, for exactitude, and for empirical grounding in the interacting relations and flows of power, their trajectories and strategies.

Lastly, the early twenty-first century is a new period in which we face questions and political realities that Niebuhr did not face and that Sheehan, of course, could not discuss in a book published in 1996. These realities and questions challenge the notion of a balance of power between nation-states.

---

40. *FH*, 130.

Human Nature, Interest, and Power

In *Reinhold Niebuhr and Christian Realism,* Robin Lovin—who is in my view among the most thoughtful of current realists and one of our finest interpreters of Reinhold Niebuhr—attempts to think about what balance of power means in a post-Niebuhrian world in ways that I find quite helpful, particularly the way he modifies the concepts of realism and the balance of power.[41] Thus it is to Lovin's analysis that I turn next.

ROBIN LOVIN: THE NEW REALITIES OF THE TWENTY-FIRST CENTURY

Lovin's analysis begins with a description of new global and political realities that impact realism generally and the notion of balance of power in particular. Among these realities Lovin names the role of terrorism since 1991, the post–Cold War globalization of commerce, the emergence of powerful trading blocs that do not match ideological borders, increases in flows of ideas resulting in the inability of political agents to control information and monopolize means of persuasion, the enhanced ease with which print media, films, and Internet transmissions travel across national boundaries, the proliferation of identities beyond those of country and/or ethnicity, and the post-9/11 resurgence of religious identity.[42] Lovin highlights some of the most salient characteristics of the new global system that comprise the context of contemporary politics and international relations. He carefully elaborates these characteristics and the implications thereof by way of specifying how the very fabric of political life has changed since the mid-twentieth century, which was the crucible in which Niebuhr's political ideas were formed.

Lovin argues that among the most notable of these shifts is the increased permeability of international boundaries.[43] This is not to say that boundaries are becoming passé, but to note the changing nature of boundaries. No longer are sovereign nation-states the primary agents for setting the terms of the global order. While the state is hardly relegated to the role of bystander, new forces in the economy, culture, and religion work to blur national boundaries by introducing boundaries that tend instead to be nonlocal, globalized, and changing. One of the upshots of this shift, then,

---

41. See Lovin's *RNCR*. This is an earlier volume than the one we will be using here that addresses criticisms of Niebuhr and anticipates new directions in realist thought.

42. *CRNR*, 38.

43. Ibid., 17.

is that state sovereignty now represents not the singular or primary locus of politics and international relations, but one among several loci—hence Lovin's identification of a "new realism" that is able to engage the multiple new loci of highly differentiated, rather than strictly consolidated, dynamics of power.

A core characteristic of the new realism for which Lovin argues is the importance of attending to multiple and highly differentiated centers of power, or what Lovin refers to as "contexts." Lovin conceives of contexts as "places of responsibility" from which action can be taken.[44] According to Lovin, as the flow of communication increases and becomes more highly differentiated, contexts generate forums. Whereas contexts tend to be local in character (even as they do not necessarily respect the boundaries of nation-state sovereignty), forums are not necessarily local. Lovin explains that a forum "transcends the specific events and locations in which discussions actually happened." Because of the broader and nonlocal character of these forums, they open up a new and larger arena of "purposes and values" that influence the conversations in that range of institutions that make up these new contexts. Further, a certain kind of "integrity" necessary to these contexts originates and is supported in them so that they develop traditions, norms of discourse, and rational criteria of their own.[45] While these forums develop their own rules of procedure, etc., they must also remain open to claims and input from other contexts and forums.

In short, Lovin's argument is that long-standing conceptions of the balance of power are no longer capable of insuring order in the contemporary globalized world.[46] He contends that the emergence and rapid acceleration of globalization means that it is now necessary to set aside the idea of a balance of power sustained by nuclear superpowers like the United States or the former USSR, and to pursue instead "a balanced relationship between global contexts" not unlike the kind of pluralism found in "successful modern states." According to Lovin, the new global order can no longer be seen as simply balancing the power of one state against another; rather, new approaches must be found that connect national governments

44. This is Robert Benne's phrase (Benne, *Ordinary Saints*, 63, quoted in Lovin, *CRNR*, 100). Lovin states that "they are settings in which from a theological point of view responsible action is possible because the command of God can be received in its immediacy and directness and specific goods, understood in specific social and historical settings, can be created and maintained."

45. *CRNR*, 134.

46. Ibid., 173.

to many other factors in the growing complexity of the emergent worldwide system.[47] Because politics has broadened in these ways, it can no longer be conceived of as confined strictly to the work of government. Lovin advocates a new kind of political realism able to accommodate and respond to the highly differentiated and globalized nature of contemporary political life. He argues that the new realism must be premised on a recognition that people appraise their long-run interests in encompassing doctrines that shape their conduct and what they yearn for across the full spectrum of their lives. These actions and hopes include what they expect from their government and its politics. Clearly this is not a twentieth-century world.[48]

Although Lovin is a significant interpreter of Niebuhr, his proposal of a new realism, one more concerned with the balance of contexts and their forums than with the balance of power among sovereign states alone, represents a major shift. I find the analytical attention Lovin pays to contexts and forums particularly persuasive and generative because they open up a way to move into the more micro and macro levels of power analysis, not only at the national and international levels. I suspect that Lovin would agree that contexts existed well before the current era of globalization but that, previously, contexts tended to be understood as even more local and less differentiated, and certainly not worldwide in their reach as they are today. I contend that just as contexts needed more attention and understanding in the ways that they shaped dynamics of power before, so do they now with the advent of globalization.

At the same time—necessarily, I would say, given the level of discourse in which Lovin is engaged—I contend that until we move directly into the specific discourses, practices, and technologies that are operative in them, contexts and forums remain quite abstract. In other words, it is not enough to recommend balancing contexts in general. In fact, quite frankly, I find the complexities of power in these highly differentiated contexts and forums so enormous that I wonder whether conventional ideas like "balance" or "equilibrium" are adequate even as applied to talk about what is going on or what is desired in the midst of such complexity. This situation was difficult enough when dealing with Niebuhr, who mentions any number of forms and types of power that operate at every level of a society, within communities, and at the international level as well. Given power's unfixed character in Niebuhr's thought, it was difficult enough to understand what

---

47. Ibid., 178.
48. Ibid., 144f.

"balance" and "equilibrium" actually meant or looked like. In the new, more complex realities of global contexts, I am even less sure of what such things mean. While I agree with Niebuhr (and, I suspect, with Lovin) that power is ubiquitous in human life, it seems to me that concepts of "balance" and "equilibrium" must be either abandoned or used very carefully with specific characteristics.

In such a situation it seems to me that new metaphors are required. For instance, rather than Niebuhr's go-to metaphors of balance and equilibrium, I think of the notion of flow. The metaphor of flow highlights how power moves in, through, and between various relationships and settings, including contexts as Lovin describes them. I mean here the examination of discourses and practices to determine their effects, and the impact of these effects on other discourses and practices. Working at the micro level and doing an ascending analysis, one might examine flows with power especially in terms of the "volume" of their movement. By volume I mean the mass, the amplitude of these effects—that is, exploring flows from multiple contexts, the range of their discourses, practices, and technologies, the scale of their relationships, the intelligibility and impact of their discourses, and so on. My point is that these "new realities" require the examination of power in radically new ways, an approach informed by the views of Foucault and dedicated to a close examination of power through an ascending analysis that certainly addresses micro relations but that can also come to more powerfully descriptive accounts of macro relations as well.

With this said, we can look at one more account of the new situation in the twenty-first century, that of Philip Bobbitt. The new market-state that Bobbitt forecasts will bring great changes in the dynamics, flows, and volumes of power.

PHILIP BOBBITT: THE NEW MARKET STATE

In his study of the history of the nation-state over the last five hundred years, Philip Bobbitt argues that a "market-state" has emerged in the past two decades in the West and around the world. This market-state no longer structures a world market. Rather, the market is now transnational and in a host of ways functions "independently of states." With this a strange reversal takes place: "the state is evaluated on whether its workforce has the necessary skills, and whether its infrastructure has been suitably configured to attract the multinational corporation."[49]

---

49. Bobbitt, *Shield of Achilles*, 221.

Human Nature, Interest, and Power

On Bobbitt's account, the nation-state can no longer guarantee security for its citizens from the threat of weapons of mass destruction, nor can it adequately command its own economy or currency, nor can it any longer shelter its culture and forms of life from the display and presentation of a host of "images and ideas"—no matter how alien, insulting, or outrageous they may be—available through an increasingly vast array of media. Add to this the host of global dangers like depletion of the ozone layer, global warming, contagious epidemics, and terrorism. Yet, Bobbitt observes, the role of the nation-state prior to this time has been to warrant national security, domestic order through law, economic growth and financial stability, and international peace and equality.[50] All of the threats just mentioned—and more that I cannot detail here—result in the loss of the credibility and legitimation of the state as that agent able to address the commonweal of its citizens. If the nation-state gained legitimacy by its capacity "to serve the welfare of all the people," the market-state "exists to maximize opportunities enjoyed by all members of society."[51]

One may well argue with Bobbitt on any number of the points that he makes, but his argument that the nation-state is in crisis seems justified. My concern is the impact of the crisis of the nation-state and the emergent market-state on the concept of the balance of power. The range and multiplicity of forces, the complex global relations, the struggle of states with their own peoples as well as with other states, the moves and thrusts of a global capitalism (and specifically its capacity to influence, if not buy off, government representatives, officials, and policymakers), the movements of populations across national boundaries, the financial crises of boom-and-bust economies, and the growing threat of eco-devastation, to cite a few examples, raise serious questions about the notion of balance. In such a complex fray, what does it mean to aim for "balance"? To be sure, nonreciprocal power certainly operates in the global context of today, but to address such complexities, and to do so concretely and materially, a decidedly different notion is required.

To sum up my comments on the work of Lovin and Bobbitt, my argument gains some support from a Niebuhrian interpreter such as Robin Lovin, who contends that in the new realities of a global system we need to examine the balance of contexts rather than a balance of power among nation-states. While I disagree with his use of balance in a framework of

---

50. Ibid., 228.
51. Ibid., 229.

that complexity, nevertheless Lovin's historical understanding of the concept of the balance of power and his efforts to examine "new realities" are quite important moves in the Christian realist position. Furthermore, Bobbitt's account of the crisis of the nation-state and the emergence of the market-state raises the most serious kinds of questions about the adequacy of the concept of the balance of power. We need not only new images and metaphors but also concepts more descriptively adequate to the complexities we now face.

CONCLUSION

There is no question that Niebuhr's analysis of power was insightful and important. But I have tried to show that when this view of power is used to analyze contemporary situations, it is imprecise, unwieldy, and, ultimately, limited in its analytic potential. In the end, Foucault's notion of power yields a more productive analysis of contemporary political dynamics. Niebuhr sees power growing out of the vitalities of the self and the necessary organization and cohesion of society and its differentiations; Foucault sees the self as a subject-agent that is produced in the strategic relations of force in a form of life. Niebuhr understands power as essentially synonymous with energy, whereas Foucault understands power as a *relationship* of energy or force or effects. So the differences between the two thinkers reside not only in their different concepts of the self and the subject, but in this very basic difference in understanding power—what it is, how it works, and what it does. The concept of the balance of power stands firmly at the center of Niebuhr's social and political thought. I call this concept into question, suggesting that the very notion of balance itself is problematic, dependent as it is on a Newtonian metaphor. Alternatively, Foucault's understanding of power works with notions of the flows and trajectories of power as primary metaphors, far more useful to describe today's power dynamics. Further, it is important in approaching the issue of power to avoid the abstract character of so many concepts used in relationship to it, especially by Niebuhr. Here again, I find Foucault very helpful in his "ascending" analysis of power, which begins in the discourses and practices of power in a specific time and place. Such an approach aids an analysis that seeks concreteness and more compelling description in the operations of power. This effort does not exclude macro forms of power, but rather addresses these in the discourses and practices of a given form of life at the level of large-scale events, among others. Not only can this approach bring more material description, but it offers rich opportunities for exploration and research as seen in Mahmood's work and, as we shall see in chapter 6, in a historical study.

With this chapter I complete my critique of Niebuhr's concepts of human nature, interest, power, and the balance of power. I now move to a brief excursus on power as formation, an area neglected by Niebuhr in his work, but one of striking importance for the kind of world sketched out in our discussions on the "new realities" of today's national and international context.

5

Internal Power

A Brief Excursus on Formation in Niebuhr

IN THIS CHAPTER I take a brief excursus to examine the relationship between power and formation. The formative capacities of power are an essential ingredient to the building of a community that can be alternative to the culture in which it exists. For those like me who understand it to be necessary for the church to stand in some tension with any culture in which it finds itself, attention to this matter must not be avoided. Yet, this topic is hardly addressed by Reinhold Niebuhr.[1]

---

1. In an e-mail from Larry Rasmussen on March 21, 2012, I received this corroborating comment about Niebuhr: "That he paid almost no attention to the formation of human character and conduct is a huge hole, given his profound understanding of human nature. We who did PhDs at Union with Niebuhr, Bennett, Shinn, et al. had to go elsewhere for that, and often didn't realize what we were missing until we set about teaching. The Union faculty all *assumed* formed Christian conscience and saw their task to be rallying that conscience for the great social issues of the day—civil rights, war and peace, economic justice, etc. Incidentally, and on your point about RN on church, there was an agreed-upon division of labor at Union. RN had become such a public intellectual that John Bennett took leadership in relating Christian realism to the ecumenical church while Reinhold, always a church person and one who loved to preach above all, moved in secular circles. We get little ecclesiology from RN as a result." Rasmussen's italics.

Human Nature, Interest, and Power

ASAD ON AUTHORIZING DISCOURSE

To demonstrate the significance of formation in a tradition of faith, I begin with Asad's work on authoritative discourse, tradition, and, in a revisit from chapter 1, habitus. Asad works with Foucault's understanding of power, but he situates it within the context of tradition, developing his conception of power in terms of what he calls an "authorizing discourse."[2] With these two areas of study Asad opens up important additional considerations in the analysis of power, which raise issues not adequately considered by Niebuhr. First I will summarize Asad's approach to authorizing discourse, and then I will turn to his understanding of tradition and its place in internal power.

For Asad power has both internal and external dimensions. Power concerns "what we do to ourselves" (internal power) and "what we do to others" (external power). His conception of power attends to these two dimensions because, on his view, power cannot be reduced simply to an "external force" but also must be seen as an "internal relationship," as "potentiality, the ability to do something," "to enact something, in connection with other persons, things, institutions, or whatever." For Asad, power concerns "how one is able to do certain things," including the ability to persuade one's self as well as others.[3] This internal dimension of power cannot be reduced to either coercion or persuasion (although both of these can be involved in authorizing discourse). Asad contends that power must not be understood "merely as struggle." Neither must it be understood only as "the clash or imposition of (external) forces."[4]

Asad's work on power focuses on the capacity of the subjects to subjectivize themselves, that is, their "making/remaking themselves or others over time." Asad characterizes these processes as both physical and somatic (hearing-feeling-seeing-remembering). These processes are more than practices of communication such as reading, conversation, etc., taken alone. Rather, authoritative discourse requires *ritual* understood as an embodiment, as "the embodiment of conviction." Carried out in communal settings it structures relationships through ritualistic practices of thinking and acting that involve "a multiplicity of material components."[5]

---

2. *PSM*, 179.

3. Ibid., 271.

4. Ibid., 214f. Here the closeness of Asad's understanding of power to Foucault's is quite clear.

5. *PSM*, 214.

The form of power involved in a subject or subjectivizing self presupposes interconnection—certainly that of subjects who are connected to one another, as well as of subjects in relationship to things, both animate and inanimate. Asad explains that subjectification takes place through "the way the living body subjectifies itself through images, practices, institutions, programs, objects—and through other living bodies." Through these means, the subject literally comes into being, taking on a distinctive character with its virtues and vices.[6] Understood this way, authoritative discourse is not externally imposed *on* the subject. Instead, authoritative discourse is more like obedience. Asad describes it as "a compelling way to live."[7] As such, it is a subject's "inner binding" and elicits "willing obedience" rather than coercive regimentation.

In his approach to authorizing discourse, Asad critically appropriates philosopher Alasdair MacIntyre's work on the concept of tradition.[8] In his important book *After Virtue* MacIntyre defines "a living tradition" as "an historically extended, socially embodied argument . . . [that is] about the goods which constitute that tradition."[9] While Asad does not question the importance of argument in tradition, he focuses on tradition in terms of practice and performance. For Asad, traditions consist in instruction in the reason for a practice and the correct way to perform a practice so that it becomes embodied in one's self. In a tradition, the subject is formed by disciplines and is responsible to authorities or master practitioners in that discipline. A crucial contention for Asad is that tradition is not primarily externally imposed onto unwilling or resistant subjects, but is "compelled from inside."[10] It forms subjects who genuinely *want* to master a tradition.[11]

6. Ibid..

7. Ibid., 234f.

8. *PSM*, 234f. I report Asad's critique of MacIntyre here on the issue of tradition as argument and as embodied. Asad also raises question with MacIntyre's view of temporality. See *PSM*, 286–88. Asad recognizes a tension between genealogy, a method he uses from Foucault, and tradition, and addresses this tension. See *PSM*, 233–35. He is responding here to an important probing of this relationship by David Scott (Scott, "Tragic Sensibility of Talal Asad," 134–53).

9. *After Virtue*, 222.

10. *PSM*, 234f.

11. But Asad appreciates MacIntyre's contribution at the point of the diversities of interpretation within a tradition and of tradition as a "space of argument." Because of MacIntyre, at least in part, Asad sees tradition as more characterized by change, more affected by time, and more "open-ended." He sees tradition as "concerned with the conditions that produce meanings" and asserts that disciplines within a tradition cultivate

Closely joined to both authorizing discourse and tradition is the concept of habitus, which I discussed in chapter 1. There we saw that habitus has to do with the cultivation of the subject's sensibilities, passions, senses, dispositions, etc. Conceived as an embodied capacity, it is an ardent and zealous performance of an embodied ethical sensitivity. A particular habitus is not something one elects or adopts, but rather is that which constitutes a subject's identity and the format of one's actions.

The ideas of authorizing discourse, tradition, and habitus constitute important forms of power in Asad's thought. They are means by which internal power operates and, as such, takes on an external power. In other words, these three can be said to comprise the capacity to form and enact agency both personally and corporately. These powers of constitution and formation have considerable impact in their capacity to build resistance to domination by the wider society and their capacity to form an alternative community to that society.

FORMATION IN NIEBUHR

I relate Asad's notion of the constitutive elements of internal power that form the subject because I find this kind of power virtually ignored in Niebuhr. In fact, I find the whole issue of formation of the self almost entirely absent in his writing. In the following comments, I will use the word *formation* rather than repeat authorizing discourse, tradition, and habitus, not only for a more economic phrasing, but also so that I do not hold Niebuhr responsible for not using Asad's concepts, which were developed well after Niebuhr's life. In particular, Niebuhr neglects even a general notion of the formation of people in the Christian faith.

I am not the first to suggest that Niebuhr tends to paint in extraordinarily broad strokes that omit crucial details when it comes to Christianity and the church. In fact, Niebuhr is often accused of ignoring the church in his writings, an accusation not well founded in light of D. B. Robertson's selective collection of Niebuhr's essays on the church, *Essays in Applied*

---

dispositions, attitudes, thoughts, desires, and behavior. Traditions nourish virtues; they form subjects. Not committed only to the past, traditions are also concerned with the future. They deal with the way limits are constructed and develop new and reworked approaches in their discourse and practice. New narratives, different virtues, and new stories develop within traditions and provide ways to "cultivate oneself or to help others cultivate themselves—without which there is no continuity in social life." *PSM*, 289.

Christianity, which runs to almost 350 pages.[12] Yet a close reading of this text reveals very little attention to the issue of formation in the church or in Christian life.

Just a few examples will suffice. First, in a discussion of "pietistic individualism" Niebuhr indicates that it did generate "disciplined and responsible individuals" but that it became only "indirectly relevant" and even then was "a source of illusion" in its interpretation and approach to justice.[13] So in this brief reference the discipline of responsible individuals lacks relevance to justice and contributes to illusion.

Second, in a discussion of Billy Graham he criticizes "an individualistic approach to faith and commitment" and cautions against making too much of the difference between the "saved" and the "unsaved." He calls for a greater apprehension offered by classical Christian faith, the Reformation, and "better still the biblical truths about the precariousness of the virtues of the redeemed."[14] This does not seem to convey any great confidence in the development of virtue in the church, and while "the redeemed" clearly require critique, this does not really address the capacities of formation.

The most extended discussion of discipline and virtue in these writings on the church occurs in a commencement address on the security and hazard of the Christian ministry delivered at Union Theological Seminary in 1957. He begins his speech by affirming that the gospel of Christ is expressed essentially in the cross, which represents both "perfect love" and "the perfect good." In Christ, then, is both "our norm and law."[15] But when he turns to discipline and virtue—as close as anything I can find to formation in his work on the church—he so qualifies his comments that I wonder how formation could have much of a role at all. Though he acknowledges that the process of growth requires "a combination of discipline and freedom, of law and grace," he moves immediately to a stringent qualification of both discipline and virtue. We are told we must not "interpret the gospel merely in terms of discipline, and particularly if we identify law and discipline with the conventions of society."[16]

Surely we need not disagree with Niebuhr on this point, but it is significant that this comment occurs in an onslaught of qualification about

12. Niebuhr, *Essays in Applied Christianity* (1959).
13. Ibid., 127.
14. Ibid., 130.
15. Ibid., 132.
16. Ibid., 135.

discipline and virtue. Niebuhr tells us that virtues are fragmentary; that all achievements—including those of virtue—are challenged by the gospel; that we must resist "premature satisfactions" with our achievements and virtues; that care is required not to fall into otherworldliness; that we must avoid "capitulation to perfection"; that the dangers of legalism, fanaticism, and building on a wrong foundation—that is, not Christ—are ever present; that traditions and conventions both "express and corrupt" the necessary disciplines of life; that their traditions and conventions must be "subject to the law of love"; that we must heed the dangers of fanaticism, conventionality, and Romanticism; and that we must never "invest a proximate good with absolute authority."[17] In short, although Niebuhr mentions growth and clearly sees growth as desirable, his elaboration of *how*, exactly, growth takes places falls far short of elaboration or elucidation. He seems clear about all the things growth must not be confused with but says precious little about what it is or what it actually *does* (or can) involve.

My impression is that virtue and discipline have "died the death of a thousand qualifications." To be sure, Niebuhr acknowledges that discipline is necessary, but where are the *constructive* suggestions for how the church is formed by "the norm and law of love" in Niebuhr's terms? Where are the practical and concrete suggestions for how the norm and law of love can be embodied and enacted? They are not there! Again, my point is not that any of his qualifications are wrong as such but simply that, given all these qualifications, cautions, and prohibitions, Niebuhr leaves his readers without any substantive suggestions for the constructive, appropriate formation of discipline and virtue. In the end, Niebuhr has none to offer, and so it would not be remiss to wonder if there is any place in Niebuhr's thought for the formation of the church through discipline and virtue as an alternative to the established culture. Niebuhr, who is open to the responsibilities of working in the fragmentary, ambiguous, and contingent "realities" of power, seems so utterly stringent in his qualifications of discipline and virtue that I wonder if his comments about the necessity of discipline and its role in growth are little more than declarations.

Finally, with Niebuhr's interest in power realities, readers might wonder why there is not greater attention to formation, this internal form of power in the church. Perhaps this neglect of formation grew out of the relative unimportance in Protestant circles of forming a body constituted as an alternative to the world during the years of Niebuhr's career. Alternatively,

---

17. Ibid., 133–36.

perhaps, it was his assessment of the unlikelihood of such a possibility given his keen sense of the accommodation of the church to the society of his time, or even the central role of meaning in his theology.

I have not developed the role of meaning in Niebuhr's thought in this essay, but a brief comment seems to be in order. Langdon Gilkey gives a very helpful overview of the centrality of meaning in Niebuhr's work. Without attempting a full summary of Gilkey's discussion, it is enough in this context simply to lift up a few of the central claims from Niebuhr. For example, meaning is not the only gift of religion, according to Niebuhr, but it is the main one. Meaning provides "a vision for the whole of history" and concerns "the most fundamental issues for existence and for reflection on existence."[18] Further, meaning is central to Niebuhr's Christology—as, for example, when he maintains in reference to Christology that meaning is disclosed in history but not fulfilled there, and that meaning comes into history only to be crucified.[19] Surely this is enough to suggest the profound importance of meaning in Niebuhr's understanding.

The kind of emphasis Niebuhr placed on meaning in his theology tends to the neglect of formation and embodiment in an explicit sense. This is particularly the case when discipline and virtue are so heavily qualified.[20] Be that as it may, this is strange in Niebuhr when one pays attention to the rich piety in his prayers and sermons. He was himself a deeply formed Christian, a man of enormous—perhaps excessive—discipline, and one characterized by an array of virtues. I can only wish that he had directed some of his intellectual power and embodied capacities to how such things came to be.

But my basic point here is one about power, and in particular what Asad calls internal power. The internal power of the Christian life, or formation, deserves attention, especially by communities of faith whose being in the world is to be understood as at least in tension with that world, and hence as an alternative to it. I believe that Niebuhr could have helped us a great deal on this point, but he did not.

Thus far, I have raised critical questions with Niebuhr's view of human nature, interest, and his concepts of power and of the balance of power.

18. *ON*, 53–55. See also 75f.

19. *NDM2*, 288.

20. As another example of my point here about Niebuhr's lack of confidence in the role of the church as a community of formation, see the last two pages of *MNHC*, 124f., certainly an important placement.

Human Nature, Interest, and Power

Further, I have questioned the absence of formation in his thought. One of my criticisms of Niebuhr is that he is not empirical enough. It is time to offer a specific case study in order to suggest a more appropriate way to study power in a historical situation, one that can focus more concretely on the discourses and practices of that setting.

6

A Narrative Illustration

HISTORIAN JON E. WILSON tells the story of a peasant uprising in 1783 in Rangpur District in Bengal, India. Governed by the English East India Company, the peasants of this district revolted against their landlords and governors, protesting the raising of their rent and coercive practices of collection. They incinerated the offices of the government and of their landlords, slayed revenue officials, and destroyed official state records. With that, the peasants proceeded to name their own leaders and initiated a government of their own. The uprising was halted when a detachment of Company troops attacked a rebel camp and killed sixty of the peasant insurgents.[1]

Aside from assessing the straightforward facts, how can we understand what happened in this peasant uprising? More specifically, what was the nature of the dynamics of power that were at play? In the pages that follow, I want to consider two possible interpretations of this revolt: first, from a Niebuhrian perspective and then, second, from Wilson's own analysis of the power relations in the Rangpur District, the uprising, its suppression, and its aftermath. The juxtaposition of these two readings demonstrates how Niebuhr's view of human nature, self-interest, and power can be used to interpret what was going on in the revolt. I then offer a counter-interpretation to Niebuhr's perspective, which will illustrate the points I have made in my critique of Niebuhr, particularly regarding his general tendency toward abstractions that cover over key social dynamics that need to be

1. Wilson, "Subjects and Agents," 180–205.

accounted for and, more specifically, the analytic problems one encounters when trying to apply his conception of power to actual historical situations.

THE RANGPUR DISTRICT REVOLT IN A NIEBUHRIAN PERSPECTIVE

As we saw in chapter 1, Reinhold Niebuhr maintains that an in-depth social analysis of politics and of power relations must be developed in terms of the dynamics of the self, which he understood as a composite of spirit and nature, and as finite but also transcendent due to the self's capacity to make an object of itself. For Niebuhr, this dialectical character is the very essence of the self. Further, the tension between transcendence and finitude generates an anxiety in the self that is ineradicable. This anxiety becomes the occasion/temptation for the self to escape its transcendence or finitude through either the overreach of arrogance or the underreach of sloth. More than that, these dynamics are compounded in human group life, in part because even the capacity of the self for self-sacrifice can be swept up into the most demonic and selfish egoism of human group life. Further, the will to power—fueled by the vitalities and forms of the spirit and nature of the self—is a basic form of the arrogance or pride of the self in which the strong seek to secure themselves against the vicissitudes of life and the loss of privilege, while the weak seek to gain security against their vulnerabilities. Hence, any genuinely Niebuhrian analysis must begin with an analysis of how the involved parties share this existential condition and these dynamics of the self.

The relevant parties to be analytically accounted for in this case are the peasants, the landlords, and the government officials. As a dominant group, the landlords possess power and privilege on a Niebuhrian view. They use their power to sustain their privilege, standing, and domination over the peasants—for example, by supporting violent action to regain the status quo that existed prior to the peasant uprising. They pursue their self-interest in and through the arrangements they have with the British colonial regime and in their relationships with the peasants. Meanwhile, the government officials have the responsibility for sustaining social order and for seeing that this situation does not devolve into anarchy. The government therefore primarily serves the interests of the landlords and seeks security and order consistent with these landlords' interest and privilege. And yet, as we shall see, the government officials understood that any number of pragmatic

A Narrative Illustration

considerations had to be taken into account if they were to rule effectively in a setting with serious divisions between landholders and peasants. The peasants, far more committed to a traditional way of life in Rangpur, approached the issues of work, property, relationships with landholders and with the government in a quite different way. They truly were other to the landholders and government officials and probably were never understood adequately by either, as we will delineate below.

In Niebuhrian terms there is a clear imbalance of power. The landlords and the government dominate the peasants and pursue their common self-interests as the backdrop to and central tension of this uprising. At the same time, the peasants' revolt is a challenge to the power of the government and the landlords. It represents an assertion of peasant self-interest against the oppression they endure.

In a Niebuhrian analysis the parties in this conflict share a common human nature. All are constituted of an ongoing dialectic of spirit and nature, of form and vitality. Each person shares an existential anxiety growing from the tension in the self between transcendence and finitude. These dynamics are compounded in group life and lead to pride and the will to power. The peasants, at times pressed into sloth by the powerlessness and oppression they endure, nevertheless in this instance see themselves possessing the power to revolt and change the arrangements under which they suffer. Meanwhile, the landlords in their own arrogance and ideological justification defend their self-interest and pressure the government to repress the peasants. And the government officials, protective of their own power and associated interests, respond violently and effectively, possessing the kind of armed force necessary to put down the rebellion.

A Niebuhrian assessment could well argue that the peasant uprising was naïve (i.e., lacking realism) due to the overwhelming force at the government's disposal and its vested interest in sustaining power over the peasants. Further, a Niebuhrian could argue that the peasants overestimated their own power and misread their options and chances of success. Moreover, this uprising and the response of the government and the landlords could be understood from a Niebuhrian perspective to demonstrate once again that a relative justice cannot be secured in a situation where power is so unequally distributed.

One may quarrel with my sketches of how the possibilities for Niebuhrian analyses of this situation could proceed, and I am by no means claiming to have presented a comprehensive and exhaustive Niebuhrian treatment. At the same time, I do not think that I have distorted Niebuhr's view. The different options for a Niebuhrian rendering of the Rangpur District revolt suggest how readily a Niebuhrian approach can be applied to a situation and how easily it yields a certain explanatory power. It seems exactly right. The clarity of Niebuhr's insight into human nature, self-interest, and power can hardly be more incisive in an event such as this. Indeed, the so-called realism of a Niebuhrian analysis seems to require no further empirical examination. We can see marks of Niebuhr's existential self operative in each of these parties: the peasants, the landlords, and the government. Each of these groups pursues its self-interest; however, the superior and therefore determinative power of the landlords and the government results in a suppression of the peasants that, unfortunately, could have been predicted by any "realistic" observer of a Niebuhrian sort.

THE RANGPUR DISTRICT REVOLT FROM A WILSONIAN PERSPECTIVE

Jon E. Wilson's analysis of the peasant revolt, however, is quite different from a Niebuhrian one. He contends that attempting to understand the dynamics between the peasants, the landlords, and the Company or government by trying to discern and explicate the motives that existed within the autonomous consciousness of any one of these groups is a flawed approach. Wilson argues that methods like this cannot adequately describe the ways in which the consciousness of individual participants—indeed, their own sense of identity—is formed by his or her social engagements with others.[2] In other words, Wilson maintains that less attention should be placed on understanding the "autonomous consciousness" that made up the personal identities and motivations of the peasants, the lords, and the Company officials and that analytical attention should be focused instead on understanding the relationships that obtained *between* the groups in this situation.[3] Wilson's analysis therefore explores how the key subjects involved saw themselves and understood the conflict.

Crucially, Wilson argues that the peasants did not conceive of themselves as "autonomous creators of a counterhegemonic social order." They understood themselves more as "interlocutors and critics of an authority" to whom they were clearly subject. That is, though they were subject to the

2. Ibid., 185.
3. Ibid., 186.

authority of the landlords and, ultimately, the colonial government officials (and did not dispute their subordinate position), they nevertheless believed that they had the capacity to "reform and amend" the authority to which they were subject in accord with their own aims. The peasants therefore understood the rebellion as an attempt to re-create good social order, not as an attempt to create an entirely novel social arrangement. Well after the revolt, they saw themselves "as supplicants and petitioners"; as the peasants said to government agents, "You are master, we are subjects."[4]

In this way, Wilson highlights that the peasants did not see themselves as powerless; and indeed, they were not completely powerless in this situation, even if they were undoubtedly subordinate. In eighteenth-century Bengal there was more land to farm than there were laborers to do the farming, and the peasants knew that the landholders were dependent on them for the labor they provided. The peasants understood that they could withhold rent or move out of the district, thereby undercutting the landowners' economic well-being. In fact, Wilson argues that the peasants believed they "inhabited a shared social world" with the landlords and regarded the labor they performed as a commodity to be exchanged for the landlords' provision of protection and economic support. Thus, according to the peasants' view of the normative social order, their labor was something like a gift. The landlords' authority was constituted on the basis of this gift of labor, and its continuity was contingent on maintaining the basic economic and social conditions the peasants needed in order to survive. The peasants believed that the landlords' power began with them—it flowed from them, to the landlords, and then back to them again, albeit in a conditional form. In short, they clearly understood that the landlord's power over them, although real, was not absolute, but ultimately and essentially relied on the labor that they provided.

The peasants' understanding of the situation was not shared by either the landlords or the colonial government. The Bengal landholders viewed the peasants instrumentally, as tenants and subjects. They understood the protection they provided to the peasants mainly as a means to sustain their authority locally. In other words, the landlords' perceptions of the nature of the relationship between them and the peasants was elitist and, quite simply, was not centrally concerned with their subject-tenants' well-being beyond how it propped up their authority.

4. Ibid., 185.

The landlords' instrumental interest in the peasants notwithstanding, Wilson reports that the landlords' "elitist idioms of self-constitution" were seriously tempered by the practical fact that the authority of the landholders required "a dialogic relationship" with the peasants who were subject to them. Put differently, even as they used nondiplomatic methods to sustain their dominant role, the landlords nevertheless had to make concessions to the peasants in order to forestall a rebellion by what was, in fact, "an armed body of the rural population" or, alternatively, the possibility of mass migration. The landholders therefore knew that to keep the peasants in their place, they had to demonstrate receptivity to compromise and readiness to dialogue with them. In fact, records indicate that the landlords frequently complained to the colonial power (i.e., the East India Company) about *its* hesitance to use coercive means against the peasants.

Turning to the colonial regime, Wilson contrasts its position with that of the peasants and the landholders. The latter groups were conscious of the fact that their capacity to act was relationally constituted—that is, that it required the cooperation (even if reluctant) of the other group—rather than absolute. The power of the landlords and peasants was not equal, but there was awareness on both sides that the collaboration of the other was essential. By contrast, the discourse and actions of British officials indicate that "they took for granted their ability to act autonomously to a far greater degree" than did the peasants and landholders. From the view of the colonial government, the peasant rebellion warranted the use of suppressive violence because the peasants' actions threatened the very social order that the Company was established to protect. And, indeed, while some landholders took issue with the repressive actions of governmental revenue agents and objected to what they regarded as a too hasty resort to violent force by the colonial regime against the peasants, for our purposes it is important to note that no one questioned the sovereignty of the Company *or* its right to put down the peasant rebellion.[5] The tactics that it used were questioned, but its *right* to do so, and even its *responsibility*, went without saying.

Wilson observes that the very fact of the uprising indicates that, regardless of how absolute or unquestionable the colonial government understood its authority over the peasants to be, challenges to that authority *could*, in fact, be made—and even made *effectively* for a brief period of time. What is more, the peasants' challenge to the Company's authority successfully fractured what Wilson calls the "univocality of the colonial voice." For

---

5. Ibid., 187f.

instance, Wilson points to evidence that the colonial government made some concessions to "peaceful" peasants who did not join the rebellion. Also, in the middle of the revolt, one official agreed to many of the demands of the peasant rebels (even though later he went back on these promises and collected rent at the previous high rate). Most important of all, the government moved to a far more pragmatic, utilitarian approach to governing the peasants. In doing so they developed a "tactical vocabulary" which began "a process" by which government officials "continually changed" the administrative approach of the colonial rule. To do so, it "transformed the language it used to legitimate its own authority."[6] These kinds of actions demonstrate that, the colonial mindset of absolute authority notwithstanding, the reality of the situation in the Rangpur District called for "complex maneuvers and negotiations" in order to secure the "absolute authority" the colonial powers claimed for themselves. The official rhetoric and the pragmatic dictates of the situation thus did not perfectly align.

Wilson's analysis highlights that each of the three constituencies in the Rangpur District had different goals and, moreover, each used a different set of strategies to try to achieve their goals. Consequently, Wilson explains that "the move each player made in each case was fundamentally dependent on the place of all the other pieces in the game. To attribute a set of events to the 'autonomous' consciousness of one or more 'agents' is to reduce a complex, dynamic process of interaction to a static set-piece encounter in which each player has no choice but to repeat the same move time and time again."[7] Wilson's argument, in short, is that "the consciousness and actions of Rangpur's landholding class were constituted by a *process of engagement* with a complex set of social forces."[8] Analyses of the revolt that focus only on the discrete perceptions of the situation held by any single party, and that do not attend to the dynamics of interaction *between* these perspectives, will not be able to account fully or adequately for the events that transpired.

In the aftermath of the revolt and as a result of other changes beyond the Rangpur District of Bengal, a slow transformation took place across northern India in the subsequent two decades or so. Landholders began to be divested of their property and, as a result, peasants began to pay taxes directly to the colonial government. In fact, many of the changes that the

---

6. Ibid., 188–89.
7. Ibid., 189.
8. Ibid., 187. Italics mine.

revolting peasants sought were eventually put into place in the following decades. On this basis Wilson concludes that the "forms of practice and thought that transformed the subjectivity of the colonial regime between 1780 and 1840 or so were *not* 'imposed' from Britain." He maintains that these changes must be understood as born out of the sustained interactions between Britain, the Indian people, and the "cultural practices of the colonial regime." Explains Wilson, "[T]his process transformed the character of the forces that engaged with each other to produce the continually changing character of colonial rule in the Indian subcontinent."[9] Let me suggest that Wilson's historical analysis indicates the highly relational, interactive character of power even in situations of marked and massive inequalities. Wilson demonstrates in this case study that power cannot be possessed; rather, power flows in the complex relationships of a form of life. That some are, indeed, in strategic positions in such a form of life seems clear, and nonreciprocal relationships of power certainly exist, at least for a time. With these thoughts in mind, let us turn to an examination of Niebuhr's notions of human nature, self-interest, and the balance of power in the light of Wilson's study.

HUMAN NATURE, INTEREST, AND POWER

Wilson's work provides a helpful narrative by which to summarize and demonstrate the findings of this study since, as I will show, his account and analysis of the Rangpur District rebellion illustrate my critique of Reinhold Niebuhr at several crucial points. To recap briefly, Wilson rejects models of historical causality that attempt to identify and locate single sources as the definitive "cause" for particular events. According to the model that his work builds, any event or set of events is "a consequence of a process of interaction between subjects (whether conscious or not) who are constituted in different ways, each with their own conscious and unconscious tendencies and trajectories." Thus the way that particular scenarios actually transpire cannot be attributed solely to any one party, not even the one (or ones) that seem to be the most powerful, but is a result of the way in which the parties interact. Historical change, in other words, is an interactive effect.[10] What, then, are the implications of Wilson's analysis of the Rangpur

9. Ibid., 191f.
10. Ibid., 189.

District revolt and the model of historical causality with which he works for a discussion of human nature, self-interest, and power?

HUMAN NATURE

The conception of subjectivity that emerges from Wilson's work challenges the way that Niebuhr understood human nature, particularly the role that Niebuhr attributed to the existential self in the dynamics of power and his understanding of the self as a universal, primordial human nature. By contrast, the conception of the self in Wilson's study is not that of Niebuhr's "constituting self" that somehow automatically and necessarily shares a common, human existential nature. As demonstrated by the events in the Rangpur District revolt, we are able to see that the historical process and complex relations that comprise these events differently constitute the selves in Wilson's account. Unlike Niebuhr's conception, Wilson's is not one that assumes a single universally shared mode of introspection that basically determines consciousness. Wilson's conception of the self admits of various and diverse discourses, conceptualities, practices, and forms of life. Hence, in his account, the normative order of the peasants was dramatically different from the landlords' understanding of the situation and the idioms of authority that they employed. Different still from either of these was the understanding of the colonial regime.

These differently constituted selves that Wilson so vividly depicts thus call into question the existence of Niebuhr's existential self, and even the very notion of an essential, commonly shared "human nature." Wilson's work helps us see that we are not, in fact, *constituting* selves, but rather we are *constituted* subject-agents. Constituted subject-agents emerge within the frameworks of, as Saba Mahmood puts it, "a historically specific set of formative practices and moral injunctions" that are in place prior to the self. "The self" in this sense has no primordial, universal nature of the kind Niebuhr professes, but instead is socially produced *in* and *through* the discourses and the practices of a form of life. It comes out of *and* is an effect of all kinds of relations of power. Thus the subject, as what Asad calls "the principle of consciousness and experience," does not *precede* power relations but emerges *from* them.

Consequently, agency, or the ability to effect one's social world, must be distinguished analytically from subjectivity.[11] The possibility of making

11. By way of clarification, let me say that Wilson is working here, in part, with the

this distinction in any given situation requires an exploration of "the grammar of concepts," to use Mahmood's phrase, which the subject-agent inhabits. The semantic and institutional networks in which agency is set not only provide the limits within which that agency can work, but also open up specific ways of connecting to others, to things, indeed, to one's own self. In this sense, insofar as the character of the subject-agent is not a primordial universal but is contingent and historically emergent, the nature of the subject-agent is not something to be *assumed* but is actually a crucial question to be *raised*. So rather than assume some universal practice of introspection, such as Niebuhr makes primordial in the anxious, finite freedom of the self, I follow the views of Asad and Mahmood that it is necessary to *explore* practices of introspection to *describe* carefully what we find, rather than to lay upon people the dynamics of our presumption.

The concept of habitus is key to the view of the subject-agent that I am proposing. A capacity of the body that is more than physical ability alone, habitus, as I explained in chapter 1, includes the formation of sensibilities and passions and the structuring of the senses. Niebuhr's view of the self and his political realism focus continually on the role of self-interest and power in disrupting or challenging or resisting established norms. The concept of habitus, however, does not focus primarily on the tendencies of subjects-agents to transgress normative boundaries but takes as its point of departure the ways in which subjects-agents are constituted and develop out of the conceptualities, the practices, and the normative formations of a form of life. Of course, this does not rule out the possibility of resistance to social norms, but certainly places social norms in a very different relation to the subject.

To be clear, I do not doubt that a subject-agent can take on the dynamics of Niebuhr's self. My contention is that subject-agents who are thus

---

distinction Talal Asad makes between subjectivity as the "principle of experience" or consciousness, and agency as the "principle of effectivity." Asad questions what he sees as the tendency of historians and anthropologists to conflate conceptually subjectivity and agency in their work. These scholars often implicitly assume that "an analysis of *subjective* consciousness," or of experience, is sufficient to understand "the agentive power," or people's ability to effect their social world. Arguing that agent and subject "do not belong to the same theoretical universe and should not, therefore, be coupled," Asad is careful to separate methodologically conscious subjectivity and agentive power. Following Asad, Wilson not only distinguishes subject and agent, but also is reticent to avoid attributing agency (understood as *monocausal* effectivity, or "responsibility") to any single subject or collective force (i.e., the state, imperialism, class, etc.). See Wilson, "Subjects and Agents," 183. For Asad's differences with Wilson, see Asad, "Responses," 239f.

A Narrative Illustration

constituted are those with a Western, individualized, essentialized view of the self whose conceptualities, practices, and forms of life continually define that self in terms of its being repressed, suppressed, or oppressed, and therefore it requires breaking free from social definitions and norms. Said differently, such a view of the self is one that is quite at home in a *specific* historical, cultural, political, and philosophical location—namely, the discourses of the liberal nation-state and a capitalist economic order.

SELF-INTEREST

In chapter 2 I drew on Albert Hirschman's detailed history of the various meanings and usages of the concept of interest in Western thought in the last five centuries. In that discussion I situated Niebuhr's many uses of "interest" in a long line of thinkers who use the word quite variously from the late medieval period onward. I identify and discuss ten of the ways in which "interest" is used in his written corpus, arguing that Niebuhr uses this term in so many dissimilar ways that, in the end, "interest" becomes a tautology, thereby obscuring more than it clarifies. Because "interest" is often used as a label that covers over multiple impulses of "motivation in the self" and obscures the profound sociality and the immense plurality of a specific discourse, its practices, and its relationship to the forms of life in a specific time and place, I contend that if the concept of interest is to be at all helpful, it needs far more precision than what we find in Niebuhr's work. At this juncture, I turn to how Wilson's analysis provides some of the conceptual clarity regarding interest that Niebuhr lacks.

The word *interest* appears only once in the discussion by Wilson, and that in its plural form when he refers to "peasant interests."[12] He uses the word in relation to the peasants' actions to force a landlord to terminate some local official and put in his place someone "more amenable to peasant interests." Wilson's use of the word *interest* in this context suggests some advantage the peasants have in the appointment of new officials, or perhaps that the new officials connect more with their normative social order or something else.

In another place in the same discussion, Wilson reports that "different players had different goals" and made use of different strategies in order to reach their objectives.[13] The language of "players," "strategies," and

12. Wilson, "Subjects and Agents," 186.
13. In her reading of this manuscript, Yvonne Zimmerman notes that "it's striking

"objectives" certainly suggests that different groups in the situation had "interests," but it is difficult to specify exactly what an "interest" really is (or is not). Wilson indicates that "moves by players" were quite basically dependent on "the place of all the other pieces in the game." Therefore, to reduce this complex and dynamic uprising and its outcome to the autonomous consciousness of agents is to obscure what happened and to misinterpret this event. Wilson claims that "an analysis of consciousness" simply cannot account for action by "any coherent agentive-subject." He argues that "the way the subjects that participated in these events were constituted was itself the product of the contingent historical relationship between the different forces."[14] Hence to use the word *interest* in a context such as this one is to claim a complex sociality of the concept (however defined) and, by that fact, also to suggest that "interest" can and will be used in many different ways.

In yet another place Wilson discusses high abstractions such as "imperialism" and "Europe," concepts that both he and Asad challenge because they do not "exist as subject-agents, whether or not one wishes to treat them as conscious entities." No single "collective consciousness" or "common set of unconscious practices or tendencies" characterizes such abstractions.[15] Wilson contends that such concepts are "the effect of an interaction between heterogeneous power relations."[16] In the context of this larger discussion, Wilson cautions against using the concept "imperialism" to describe "a player calculating what his next move should be in a game whose stakes are familiar to all participants, and whose rules are accepted by them." The reason both Wilson and Asad reject this formulation is that it treats imperialism as if imperialism itself is "an already constituted agent" that operates in a fixed way. Wilson and Asad contend that imperialism should be understood as "a process of interaction and convergence constitutive of subjectivity rather than a process constituted by subject-agents."[17] Such an understanding of imperialism (and, indeed, of all such high abstractions in political theory) has serious consequences for speaking of national interests, unless such notions are carefully delineated and displayed in their

---

how Wilson is characterizing the situation as a 'game' with 'players'... which is different than a 'situation' in which there are 'parties' or 'constituencies.'"

14. Ibid.
15. Ibid., 200.
16. Ibid., 199.
17. Ibid., 197–98.

necessarily complex sociality. Generalized appeals to national interests take on a ghost-like quality, unless they are carefully described in terms of their use in the discourses and practices of a given time and place.

I read Wilson's metaphor of a player who calculates his or her next move as one way to think of interests. While the idea of calculating a move cannot necessarily be reduced to calculating advantage, certainly in many cases calculation of advantage would be included in the process of determining a next move. But the question Wilson's position poses is what happens to notions such as "calculation" when imperialism is seen as a complex historical process of interaction and convergence that constitutes who we are instead of as some kind of already constituted agent. In such a context, "interest" cannot be understood in Niebuhrian terms as the calculation of a constituting self who egoistically pursues her or his advantage. Instead, it makes more sense to understand interest as profoundly dependent upon the discourses, the practices, and the relationships of a form of life. In the next chapter I shall suggest that, in this sense, interests are dependent upon a tradition, rightly understood.

Moreover, interests are not rationally calculated "advantages" construed by an existential self in its egoism. Interests cannot be strictly reduced to utilitarian "benefits" in the wide variations of their use. But to the extent that interests are used in terms of advantage, even here they are more adequately described as constituted by and taking form in heterogeneous relations of power in specific locales of a form of life. Such an understanding of interest does not preclude the possibility that a subject-agent can be formed by relations of power in such a way that she or he in fact *does* pursue rationally calculated advantages. That a subject-agent might be thus formed is entirely possible. My real point, however, is to argue that the concept of interest has to be situated in the junctures of a totality of forces where subject-agents operate. Interests ought not to be relegated to the consciousness of existential selves whose egoism is compounded in group life and "taints" society and history. Like subject-agents, interests are internally constituted and externally positioned.

So the various ways Niebuhr used the concept of interest, the long history of this concept in the West, and new brain research with its findings of registers of subjectivity call us to far greater caution in using this concept.[18]

18. As discussed in chapter 2, William Connolly's work with brain research points to new directions for addressing the subject-agent, particularly his focus on different "registers of subjectivity" which involve "layered intricacies of thinking and judgment," "visceral registers of subjectivity," and pre-representational sites of appraisal. Connolly's

Human Nature, Interest, and Power

Concepts such as "interest" and "self-interest," understood as universals, have nothing like the precision that is claimed for them in terms of their ability to illuminate the various kinds of pursuits that differently situated, and thus differently constituted, subject-agents pursue in social life.

POWER AND THE BALANCE OF POWER

The narrative Wilson tells is certainly not one of a balance of power in Niebuhr's terms. Yet, it is also not quite a story where the Company or the landlords can be seen as holding complete power over the peasants. Yes, the Company can be understood as the organization of power in the state, as a Niebuhrian analysis would suggest. Similarly, the landholders and the peasants can be understood as the organization of power in the wider community. Moreover, the power clearly is not "balanced" between the landlords and the peasants. At the same time, Wilson points out that there is no sense in which it makes sense to say that any of these parties *possessed* the power in a totalizing sense.

Wilson also notes that none of these events can be attributed to some independent notion of consciousness by any one of the specific agents engaged in the revolt and its aftermath. Indeed, even more sharply, Wilson argues that an analysis of consciousness cannot explain the actions in this event. Even if understood as coherent subject-agents, none of the parties in the struggle can completely account for the dynamics of power at work. The parties of this event are not fully autonomous; they are interdependently related to one another. Thus we can see that power cannot be understood as a property that different parties either possess or lack. Instead, we can see that power is more accurately characterized as a dynamic flow *within* the strategic relations that characterize their lives *together*. This means that to try to answer the question, "Who holds the power in this situation?" raises what Foucault calls "a labyrinthine and unanswerable question."[19] No single party holds the power. Power is exercised and constituted by the relations *between* and *among* the parties. So to ask who—that is, which party—holds

---

work, moreover, opens avenues that significantly affect various uses of the concept of interest, and his use of economist Mark Blyth on the role of identity opens the way for new developments in exploring both its impact on interest, variously defined, and on the subject.

19. Foucault "Two Lectures," 34–35, 36, quoted in Wilson, "Subjects and Agents," 194.

the power implicitly presumes that "abstract, transcendent subjects" actually exist as such—a presumption that, as we have seen, is not borne out by Wilson's analysis. Wilson's case study highlights how power flows among subjects. It circulates; it operates in something like a chain or, to switch the metaphor, like "a current in an ocean."[20] Power is used and carried out in a web-like organization, to use yet another metaphor. Its dynamic is not located "in someone's possession"; it cannot be grasped or consumed like a commodity.[21] Power is exercised, used, and deployed, not held, consumed, or possessed.

It is here that I find Asad's comments about power as reported above very helpful. He characterizes power as "capability," explaining that power is not "simply the clash or imposition of (external) forces" but is also the "realization of (internal) potentiality"—an ability that assumes the complex relatedness of people and things. This capacity to act by persons and by linguistic and other inanimate things (e.g., signs or symbols) occurs within a manifold of relationships that make such events possible.[22]

Further, Asad recounts that when he became "seriously interested" in colonial history, he realized that the "dominators" and "the dominated" were what he calls "joint authors" of the "complex conditions" that began and constituted colonialism. For example, oppressed people to some extent participated in their own oppression. His point is not that each party had "the same power of decision" (clearly they did not); neither does he mean that each party was "equally innocent" in their decisions (clearly they were not). Asad's point is that the asymmetrical nature of the relations of power that comprise colonial and postcolonial power renders the existence of great numbers of people quite vulnerable to "intervention by others in a nonreciprocal way." The centrality of power in history resides not only in the sense that some leaders' decisions are able to impact so dramatically the lives of so many (whether positively or negatively); power also describes the capacity people have to affect their *own* lives (their internal power). He cites the student uprisings in the 1960s and the Kababish people as examples of the ways in which a more dominant power can be confronted by such

---

20. Foucault uses the word *chain*; see Wilson, "Subjects and Agents," 195. For the metaphor of "a current in the ocean," I am indebted to Yvonne Zimmerman, who kindly read the unpublished manuscript.

21. I am indebted in this paragraph to Wilson and his use of Foucault's view of power in "Subjects and Agents," 195.

22. Asad, "Responses," 212–13.

movements and groups, even if the students or the Kababish people were not as powerfully positioned as the dominant parties they confronted.[23]

In chapter 3 I examined Foucault's conception of power, which is central to Wilson's work. I do not need to rehearse that again here, but instead simply to register a reminder of the historicity of a concept such as the balance of power, its many uses in the history of the West in the modern period, and especially its difficulty of application in the late twentieth and early twenty-first centuries with the new realities that Sheehan, Lovin, and Bobbitt name. Further, Foucault's work is very important because of his focus on the specific discourses, technologies, and practices of power in a particular form of life in a given time and place that can be explored in both their micro and macro formations. In Foucault's focus on concrete discourses and practices we are provided with resources to resist the abstractions that mislead us by obscuring the flows of power that both form our lives and provide the means to be both subjects and agents. Further, a concept such as balance of power is a high abstraction when placed upon the dynamic and relational character of power as suggested by Foucault, Asad, Mahmood, and Wilson. That the metaphor of balance comes historically from Newtonian physics is clear. Today it hardly has the compelling descriptive power it did in another time, although even then it was not adequate to the level of analysis suggested here. We need not only greater rigor in describing the micro and macro forms of power, but we need a new metaphor for the nonreciprocal relations of power. The metaphor of balance will not do.

CONCLUSION

So how do we pull together the critique of the concepts of human nature, self-interest, and power that I have been building in terms of its applications for social thought? For one thing, it is not enough to complicate each of these concepts by displaying their genealogy and their multiple uses in the history of the West. It is also important to disaggregate their relations to each other in Niebuhr's thought. The anxious freedom of his existential self is ever tempted toward an arrogant egoism, self-regard, calculation of advantage, and, ultimately, a prideful will to power. For Niebuhr, not only was this true at the individual or micro level, but it was especially so in group life, at the macro level. Hence, the relations of human nature, self-interest,

---

23. Asad, "Trouble of Thinking," 254.

and power are tight in Niebuhr's thought. Even his alertness to the historicity of individuality in the West does not finally qualify the connections between these three major components of his thought.

I do not forget here his claims of the ways in which faith helps us cope with anxiety, or the role of norms, or the considerations of wider or more encompassing interests; nonetheless there can be little question about how inextricably connected human nature, self-interest, and power are in his thought. Further, the role of self-interest and power in violating established norms is basic to how he understands realism. For a thinker with such a gripping notion of the contingency, fragmentation, vicissitudes, and finitude of both the creation and history, it is strange indeed not only that these concepts in themselves should be seen and used with such consistency, but that their relationships together should be understood with such fixity.

Of course, I will state again that my point here is not that subject-agents do *not* have or pursue interests, variously understood. It is also not my point that subjects-agents do not pursue power, nor is it to deny that nonreciprocal relationships of power exist. My concern has been to show that when we follow Niebuhr in treating power as if it is something that can be unilaterally "possessed" by an existential, self-constituting individual whose dynamics are compounded in group life, we obscure the relational character of power. A view of power that treats it as a fixed and identifiable substance to be "had" or "balanced" obscures the way that power actually operates. So my basic problem with Niebuhr's view of power, and hence with all his social thought, is that for all his "realism," his key concepts simply do not have compelling descriptive power when one moves beneath the abstractions and examines the explicit discourses and practices of people in their concrete, lived lives. Said differently, my fundamental problem with Niebuhr is that he is not "realistic" enough.

As I said in the introduction, it is no small thing to critique the social thought of an intellectual giant like Reinhold Niebuhr, and so in the concluding chapter my task is twofold: to name the political implications that I see growing out of my critique and, closely connected to this, to identify the alternatives to his account.

7

Political Implications

THOSE WHO HAVE READ this far will, of course, recognize not only my explicit indebtedness to Foucault and to those influenced by him, but also a kind of subtext at work in these pages. My examination of Niebuhr's social theory has attempted to problematize his thought by offering alternative discourses and practices, and by the use of a method of genealogy, a methodology that, as Foucault explains, is able to "account for the construction of knowledges, discourses, domains of objects etc., without having to make reference to a subject which is either transcendental in relation to the field of events or runs in its empty sameness throughout the course of history."[1] For this reason, I have been attentive to the subtle variations of concepts over time and have been unwilling to attribute universal "essences" to them, arguing that no concept—including cherished ones in the realist tradition such as human nature, self-interest, and balance of power—has any universal and stable essence except that which accrues through its repeated use. In these ways I have tried to defamiliarize, to make strange, several of the concepts that are foundational to Niebuhr's work in light of the historicity and, therefore, the contingencies, differences, variations, and complexities of their use not only in the West but also within his own thought. In this concluding chapter I intend to suggest some of the implications growing out of this study. It is not enough, finally, to challenge Niebuhr; I must offer some alternative approach to the key issues raised regarding human nature, interest, and power. Therefore, in this chapter I will name some of the crucial

---

1. Foucault, "Truth and Power," in *P/K*, 117–18.

political implications that I believe grow from my alternative approach to these three key concepts. I turn first to the matter of subject-agent.

SUBJECT-AGENT

In chapter 1 I argued for a highly complex constituted subject that emerges in the discourses, practices, and forms of life in a given time and place as a counter-concept to Niebuhr's notion of the primordial, universal existential self. Refusing Niebuhr's dynamic of a self that makes an object of itself in the forms and vitalities of its transcendent and finite existence, I have argued for a conception of the subject that attempts to avoid binary conceptualities, that attempts to be alert to a wide variety of practices of introspection, that recognizes layers of subjectivity, and, finally, that seeks to be alert to the complex weave of sin. Such a view does not claim that there is one central or essential form of human subjectivity (i.e., a fundamental human nature) but is flexible enough to allow for and easily accommodate a great variety of subjectivities. One of the political implications of such a view, then, is that it attempts not to bring so-called universal concepts *to* subject-agents in a form of life, as does Niebuhr, but instead sees such subject-agents as opportunity for careful and close exploration.

A second political implication is a heightened sense of the "otherness" of those who live in the different forms of life that this conception of human subjectivity takes as its point of departure. In his extraordinary book on Wittgenstein, *Ethics Without Philosophy*, James Edwards suggests that Wittgenstein develops ethics as a moral sensibility that appreciates the profound mystery of the world. Edwards characterizes this moral sensibility as an ethics of love that attempts to treat the world and the other "as a mystery worthy of love."[2] With this sensibility, Wittgenstein is able to resist the impulse "to turn all mystery into a riddle, into a problem soluble with enough effort and insight."[3] For my present purposes, we can say using Edwards' language that subjects, or people, are not a riddle to be solved but a mystery before which to be astonished.

To say such a thing, of course, is to be vulnerable to the charge of romanticism and naiveté, especially in the arena of politics. So let me acknowledge that in the ebb and flow, conflict and constraint, and tactical bulldozing and retreat of politics, one simply cannot be consumed by "a

2. Edwards, *Ethics Without Philosophy*, 239.
3. Ibid., 234.

just and loving gaze directed upon an individual reality."[4] At the same time, the harm that has been done in politics in my lifetime—at every level, from local to global—by means of stereotyping, mischaracterization, and false projections onto those who are perceived as "other," the enemy, or who are otherwise subjugated and vulnerable to abuses of power is immeasurable. Further, the projection of Niebuhr's view of the self has been profoundly misused on occasion. Niebuhr often warned about the idols of one's point of view and of one's devotion to race, class, and nation. I believe that his warnings are further evidence of the work of a great mind, but in the end these warnings do not sufficiently deflect the problems of his model of the self that I have discussed. The complexities of the subject require not only the most careful explorations of the subjects in the form of life in which they emerge and are situated, but invite careful attention to and consideration of the possibilities for new avenues of action; directions for negotiation and compromise; and possibilities for law and policy that are opened up by such explorations.

Another political implication of this view of the subject resides in the issue of freedom itself. For Niebuhr, human freedom is rooted in the transcendence of the self and its capacity to make an object of itself. Without rejecting various forms of self-reflexivity, my argument, however, is that there is yet another dimension of freedom that requires much more attention than that given in Niebuhr. Specifically, I allude here to a range of practices that Asad identifies as capaciousness, suggesting by this the capacity, the resourcefulness, the know-how, the language, the skills, and the savoir faire to navigate and use effectively the discourses and the practices of a form of life.

Capaciousness involves a subject so formed in an authorizing discourse that the subject takes on agency precisely in the ability to think, speak, and move easily and expertly in a form of life. It is to know what can be said and what can be done in a particular operative regime of truth. Capaciousness involves intimate familiarity with and proficiency in the feel, the rhythms, and the temporality of a way of life. It is to possess timing, to understand location, to intuit the atmosphere of a situation, to read emotions, and to work within the dispositions and the sensibilities of a sociocultural context. In politics this kind of capaciousness is utterly essential; it is a freedom to think, to relate to people, to grasp situations, to move and to act. Indeed, I think the combination of Niebuhr's immense intellect and

4. Murdoch, *Sovereignty of the Good*, 34

Political Implications

breathtaking rhetorical skill suggest that he possessed a kind of genius in this regard, leaving me to wish he had done more to name and develop these kinds of capacities—this kind of freedom—in his own writing.

The final political implication of the constituted subject-agent considered here as an alternative to Niebuhr's existential self is that it provides a sorely needed antitoxin to the poisons of the concept of the free autonomous self. To be sure, Niebuhr also opposes this concept, but to the extent that he conceptualizes a primordial self prior to the "accidents" of race, class, culture, and history, his conceptualization of the self is still very much within the liberal political and philosophical tradition.

In U.S. culture today, the free autonomous self is generally seen as the authentic self. It is understood to be, as Daniel Bell has aptly described it, "pre-given": a self with "originary desire lurking in some uncompromised interiority."[5] Such a self therefore sees tradition as a threat to the authenticity of autonomous freedom. Tradition, in other words, is perceived as captivity, and obligation as external bondage. Thus perceived, the journey of the self is not one of *formation*, but of *discovery and identification* of the vast territories that are understood as *already* residing in the self, awaiting their revelation in the journey to "who one really is." Accordingly, the primary task of such selves is understood in terms of disclosure, not the development of capacities. Indeed, the work of the self is to free one up so that one's "authentic" being may surface and transcend the encroachments of background and culture. Dominantly a consumerist construction, this is the self that understands freedom as choice and thus displays a marked tendency toward blindness to the discourses and practices that shape it in a market-based form of life. It is this view of the self, says Sheldon Wolin, that turns the citizen into a consumer and that leads to the devolution of civic culture.[6]

The free autonomous self is a powerful fiction and a prevalent organizing narrative in American everyday life. Politically, the challenge is to outnarrate it, by which I mean to articulate a view of the subject-agent that not only calls the "truth" of this fiction into question, but that also provides a more compelling account of the role of formation in the emergence of the subject. A great deal of cultural wisdom is contained in understanding that formation, training, and skill are required for the competent performance

---

5. Bell, *Liberation Theology at the End of History*, 98. Bell describes this view of the self as "the therapeutic self."

6. Wolin, *Politics and Vision*, 588.

of a great range of activities—everything from playing baseball to repairing a car, from child-rearing to deepening a marriage, from learning a song to learning an occupation. Obviously, these capacities are not completely absent in U.S. culture, but the more dominant account of the free autonomous self seems to silence, or at least diminish, the wisdom they subtly yet consistently convey.

While this dominant account of the self requires the critique of a more cogent narration, any alternative account will ultimately fail unless embodied in an alternative form of life, by which I mean a community formed in discourses and practices that refuses the free autonomous self and develops a habitus that displays and witnesses to different sensibilities. My point is that when politics is understood as the way people organize their lives together in pursuit of the goods that form and shape who they are, such alternative communities *are* a politics. I shall say more about this in the following discussion on power, but first we need to examine the implications of our revised work on the concept of interest.

INTERESTS

By now my discussions of the variability of interests and the ways in which the concept is often reduced to a tautology may have tried the patience of some readers. Here, finally, I am ready to discuss the political implications of my critique of the notion of "interests" and to suggest where these implications lead.

Political theorist Hannah Arendt traces the word *interest* to a derivative of the Latin *inter-esse* or *inter homines esse*, suggesting that this etiology alludes to the notion of "to be among men [sic]."[7] She points out that "being among men [and women]" is inherently a situation of plurality. As she explains, "Plurality is the condition of human action because we are all the same, that is, human, in such a way that nobody is ever the same as anyone else who ever lived, lives or will live."[8] According to Arendt, plurality is not merely the *conditio sine qua non*, but the *conditio per quam* of all political life. Hence she does not use *inter-esse*, or interest, to suggest merely the pursuit of advantage or the pervasiveness of self-regard. To the contrary, she uses the word to indicate the pervasive plurality of human beings and human action. Consequently, "interest" in Arendt's conception

---

7. Arendt, *Human Condition*, 7–8, 51.
8. Ibid., 8.

involves profound sociality. Such sociality does not exclude self-regard or the rationally calculated pursuit of advantage per se, but places these very specific and particular pursuits in a frame of far more complex social and political usages.

In his study of broad-based organizing, *Blessed Are the Organized*, religious studies scholar and public philosopher Jeffrey Stout argues that most grassroots democratic organizing in the United States is premised on a complex understanding of human motivation. He contends that a narrow conception of self-interest is incompatible with organizing work because effective organizing requires attention to the complexity of human motivation and the range of its expression in everyday life. Hence, Stout points to the tradition of community organizing in this country as a site of resistance to "the reduction of politics to the negotiation of preferences and the coordination of interest groups in the narrow sense of 'interest.'"[9] For organizers who work on the ground with a broad range of grassroots people, a complex notion of interest is utterly indispensable.

Stout is not alone in attending to the complexity of the notion of interest. Political theorist Danielle Allen rejects the notion that self-interest refers to any one thing and proposes that self-interest is more accurately understood in terms of a spectrum, with rivalrous pursuits located on one end and more cooperative and equitable pursuits on the other. Allen's point is that the bonds of a political body or unit do not rely on self-interest narrowly conceived, but on a wide range of practices and cultural habits that are actually grounded in more equitable, less explicitly egocentric forms of self-interest. She believes that such "philosophical claims" are necessary to stabilize "any cultural form in which the generation of trust is to be prioritized."[10]

Whatever one may think of the basic theoretical backdrop of her point of view—that is, the role of equitable self-interest in sustaining political bonds—I find her image of a spectrum useful but inadequate to address the diverse uses of the concept of interest. While she certainly understands that interest is a complex notion, I am not convinced that the image of a spectrum is adequate to that complexity. Historically, as we saw in chapter

---

9. Stout, *Blessed Are the Organized*, 217. See 216–31 and also xvii, 41, 321 n. 119.

10. Allen, *Talking to Strangers*, 137–39. She argues that three things are necessary in order to form a culture around an equitable self-interest: self-interest must be understood to take multiple forms; the goal of sustaining the political bonds within a society or state must be understood as serving every citizen's interest; and political bonds require equitable or non-egoistic expressions of self-interest in order to survive.

2, the uses of the word *interest* do not fit into a single spectrum but require some more complex image or rendering.

In *Capitalism and Christianity, American Style*, William Connolly proposes the image of a bush in a discussion of what he calls "presumptive generosity" and "presumptive bellicosity," which he describes as the two ends of a long continuum, that is, "a long line of possibilities, with most of us having bits and pieces of each in our souls."[11] But he finds a continuum too simple because life cannot be reduced to a line. He suggests instead that these "relational dispositions" that reside within us but also between us take on the branch-like complexity of a bush. Drawing on his image I contend that the different forks and branches of a bush are analogous to the way certain usages of interest are differentiated and how some of these differentiations have basic family resemblances to one another. Major branches within the bush take a specific use of self-interest—for instance, calculation of advantage—as a primary point of departure, while still reflecting the diversities of self-interest in the other branches. Further, conceptualizing interests on the analogy of a bush permits a wider analogy of a surrounding ecosystem, or the idea that the "bush" of self-interest is situated in a larger arboretum of human motivation.

Images such as those of a spectrum or a bush are helpful tools for expanding concepts of interest, but my concern here is that an examination of the political implications of interests requires something more than analogies that are either graphic (a spectrum) or biological (a bush) to describe and engage the enormous complexity of the use of the concept of interests. For this reason, I contend that self-interest must be understood in some more encompassing narrative form. Said differently, interests seem to be inextricably embedded in story. Furthermore, specific interests are embedded in *particular* stories. Indeed, even in the wide variety of ways in which Niebuhr uses the concept of interest, each of these varieties resides in a great range of stories. It is even possible to say that the variety of ways Niebuhr uses "interest" in his work results from the larger context of enormous narrative diversity. Within this larger range of stories there is plenty of room, for instance, for calculations of advantage or motives of self-regard or enlightened self-interest; however, the great complexity of interest is not rooted in stable and universally invariable existential dynamics of the human self, but in the profoundly relational character of human social life and in the specific contexts of narrative. Wilson's case study of the

---

11. *CCAS*, 5.

Political Implications

Rangpur District rebellion (see chapter 6) and his analysis of how both the subjectivities and agencies of the peasants, the landholders, and the government were so very different from one another, and of how their respective sets of interests emerged out of the different stories of these three groups, highlighted how crucially important narrative is as the context for understanding self-interest. Indeed, it is not enough to speak of the profound sociality of interests as suggested by Arendt because sociality requires in this case a more specific engagement in narrative. Strictly speaking, sociality lacks sequence and plot.

Story is an extraordinarily helpful way in which to locate and to understand interests. The use of interest as a concept emerges within a particular story and can take on a very specific character. Yet even this is not enough, because narrative itself can seem to float free from a form of life. It is for this reason, therefore, that story *itself* needs to be placed in a larger context, namely, the context of a tradition. Stories must be located within larger traditions because the value of stories in understanding interest gains descriptive power to the extent that stories participate in and draw from a tradition.

Story, or narrative, is a central category in Alasdair MacIntyre's influential book *After Virtue*. MacIntyre argues that narrative is the fundamental and necessary "genre" for describing human actions in moral life. He develops this point in a discussion of the role of sequence in making a single action intelligible.[12] Distinguishing an intelligible action from a single action taken alone, MacIntyre argues that an intelligible action makes sense only as a possible action within a succession of actions. For example, I drive out of my way to purchase more expensive items at a family-owned hardware store because I think it morally important to support small, locally owned businesses in my community. This makes no sense apart from the larger sequence of events in which this act occurs. Further, any individual's short-term *intentions* become intelligible only when placed in the frame of some longer-term intentions, such as why I believe small businesses are important both economically and morally. The point is that my intentions

---

12. MacIntyre, *After Virtue*, 208f. I am indebted to Stanley Hauerwas for calling this passage to my attention. See Hauerwas, *Performing the Faith*, 140. Hauerwas does not, however, make my point about the relation of action and story to interest. I must be held accountable for this claim, although it does seem to follow directly. Even if the intention and assertion of a given self-interest may not be a moral action, these do not seem to escape MacIntyre's comments about the relationships between action, sequence, setting, and history.

occur in a causal and temporal order in which the reasons for my patronizing a more expensive hardware store at this time in my life make sense only by their placement in the history of this society at this time. Actions and intentions require story if they are to be intelligible.

Drawing on MacIntyre's insights, I contend that interests as intentions are to be understood in some sense as an intelligible action in a sequence in a given setting or settings in a history. Interests therefore require story for intelligibility. Even short-term and seemingly minor interests do not escape this characterization because they, too, are located in a sequence that is itself set in a history. My work over the past eleven years in community organizing has impressed on me the centrality of story. A particularly powerful exercise known as "one-on-one meetings" is one I turn to frequently. In a one-on-one meeting, two people sit down and tell each other their stories. The process and experience of sharing one's story with another person is a first step in the development of a public friendship. A public friendship is not the close personal relationship of intimate friendship, but the friendship of people as citizens actively engaged together in efforts for the common good. Narrative is also central in what are called "house meetings." House meetings are sessions with a half dozen or more people who tell their stories about what is going on in their lives in relationship to issues such as the economy, jobs, or neighborhood safety that are of concrete concern to the gathered participants.

Over and over again I have been struck by the fact that we do not typically address the issue of self-interest in a narrowly conceived sense as something that is exclusive to one individual and therefore not shareable with others. This is not to say that there is little variety to the interests that get expressed in the stories these exercises generate. In fact, the variety of interests that people have is so wide that it is impossible to narrow them to two or three fundamental uses of the concept. My argument is that the reason for this wide variety of interests that makes narrowing the possible meanings of "interest" impossible is that the interests people express are so narratively embodied that, apart from these stories, the interests would lose all discernible connection to the form of life out of which they arise and that gives these interests their intelligibility. In other words, taken out of their narrative contexts, interests become so hopelessly abstract that the individuals to whom these interests ostensibly belong would not usually recognize them as their own.[13] In abstract form, interests are not intelligible as their self-interests.

13. Jeffrey Stout in his study of democratic grassroots organizations reports that

Political Implications

I broached this topic of self-interest and story with Joe Rubio, an organizer with the Industrial Areas Foundation and the lead organizer for the Valley Interfaith Project in Phoenix, Arizona, the organizing effort with which I work. His perspective illustrates MacIntyre's philosophical account of the way that story mediates intention and action. Rubio explained, "We don't know what our interests are until we have a story." He also observed that "the intensity of an interest comes in a context." Intensity is a crucial issue for organizers, because an interest that is intensely felt offers tremendous energy to community organizers—energy that can tip the balance between an organizing effort that is deemed successful and one that never gets off the ground, despite everyone's best efforts. "Story," Rubio continued, "implicates context, and the strain of the narrative creates something different and elicits an integration, especially if that story is seen in some larger context." Rubio's comment that story implicates context is clearly in concert with MacIntyre's argument about actions and intentions and the necessity of temporal sequence, narrative, to their intelligibility.

Well known for his work on narrative in relation to theology and for his efforts in recovering virtue in theological ethics, Stanley Hauerwas is indebted to the view of story that characterizes MacIntyre's earlier work, particularly *After Virtue*. But Hauerwas observes a shift in the focus of MacIntyre's intellectual work following the publication of this book, away from narrative and toward development of an account of the role of tradition in rationality.[14] For my purposes, the shift in MacIntyre's focus from narrative to tradition—a concept that he defines in *After Virtue* as "a historically extended, socially embodied argument in part about the goods that constitute a tradition"[15]—raises questions about the role of interest within the larger context of a tradition. Often, the idea of "tradition" is understood in relation to an account of moral life, which I do not as such contest. I contend,

---

these efforts do at times begin with a more narrow view of self-interest, but that organizers "resist reduction of politics to the negotiation of preferences and the coordination of interest groups in the narrow sense of 'interest.'" See his *Blessed are the Organized*, 217.

14. Hauerwas wonders if "one of the reasons for MacIntyre's reticence to draw attention even to the narrative character of tradition might be that if MacIntyre worked to develop his account of the importance of narrative, he would not be able to talk about the importance of narrative qua narrative. Instead he would have to talk about *a* narrative, which might force him to develop his thought in ways that would require him to do something more than philosophy. That 'something else' I think is theology, which is the subject that MacIntyre has spent a lifetime avoiding." Hauerwas, *Performing the Faith*, 141.

15. MacIntyre, *After Virtue*, 222.

however, that interests also must be understood in relationship to the tradition in which they arise and are situated. Another way to say this is to point out that if one takes a MacIntyrean view of tradition as consisting "in part" of an argument through time over the intrinsic goods of that tradition, it is easy to conceive of interests narrowly and to posit them as something other than or external to these "goods," particularly when interests are expressed negatively as greed, avarice, revenge, etc. But the concept of interest cannot be reduced to such vices, as we saw in chapter 2. There are, of course, legitimate interests.

Further, in the arguments, in the complex relationships, and in the temporal sequences in the massive complexities of a tradition, there are multiple stories. Stories populate tradition and many of the stories are expressions of, deal with, and narrativize interests, quite variously understood. I am suggesting that a tradition is concerned not only with intrinsic goods, but also with interests more instrumentally and more extrinsically—yes, also selfishly—understood. That is, these are not necessarily intrinsically good, but may have to do with thinking and action by agents that represent a very wide range of moves such as advantage-seeking, self-regard, highly routinized actions, instrumentally rational efforts, as well as the kind of discourse and practice we characterize as enlightened self-interest, etc.

Another way to state my claim about the relationship of interests and tradition is that interests do not exist *prior to* or *apart from* a tradition or traditions. Interests do not have independent, existential existence. Interests are formed, take hold, and have meaning only *within* the matrix of the traditions that form subject-agents and communities. Interests are located in stories, and stories are located in larger traditions. Traditions, therefore, are the fundamental context of interests.

As we have seen, a key role that interests play for Niebuhr is in their conflictual relationship with established norms, such that self-interest can be invoked as a reason or motivation for violating established social norms. In such an understanding, are interests external to tradition? I think of King David in the Old Testament and his dalliance with Bathsheba. This story from 2 Samuel relates David's considerable stealth after getting Bathsheba pregnant; he brings her husband, Uriah, back from the battlelines for a conjugal visit so that Bathsheba's pregnancy can be attributed to him and not to David. When Uriah's loyalty to King David and to the soldiers in the field leads him to refuse to sleep with Bathsheba, David has Uriah returned to battle and placed in harm's way, a move that results in Uriah's being fatally wounded. On the one hand, David's conniving has to be among the most narrow expressions of self-interest. It violates the established moral norms of Israel's life so stunningly articulated by Nathan in his confrontation with David later in the story.

Although I mean no endorsement of David's actions, I wonder if, on the other hand, it is even possible to understand or talk about David's "self-interest" apart from the tradition in which he pursued it? In other words, does not even the very premise that David's actions grievously violated Israelite moral sensibilities make sense only in the context of the tradition in which these abuses occurred? The complex of relationships in which David pursued his self-interest and the sequences of his intentions and actions occurred in a particular context that has a unique history—a context and a set of interests profoundly shaped by the patriarchy of that time. Indeed, one need not condone an interest or a set of interests in a given setting in order to acknowledge how profoundly interests are shaped by and participate in the tradition of that setting. For this reason, to reduce tradition only to formulation of an argument over goods (which MacIntyre does not do) results in a distorted view of tradition, unless, of course, one is also prepared to grant that interests—even narrow, knifing, murderous interests—are "goods." I highly doubt this was MacIntyre's intent. As MacIntyre states, tradition is *"in part"* an argument over intrinsic goods.[16]

---

16. Some political thinkers object to this notion in another way, arguing that it is possible for the democratic nation-state to be tradition-free in the sense that it does not endorse commonly held goods. In a case like this, an agent can pursue self-interest unencumbered in a tradition-free setting. The purpose of the state is then to provide certain rights that guarantee a procedural justice but do not, as such, represent a tradition. Jeffrey Stout rejects this view, arguing that democracy *itself* is a tradition. In *Democracy and Tradition* he cites the "habits of reasoning," "attitudes toward deference and authority," "love for certain goods and virtues," and a "disposition to respond to certain types of actions, events, or persons with admiration, pity, or horror" as some of the basic characteristics of the democratic tradition, claiming that the ethical substance of democratic tradition consists in its "enduring attitudes, concerns, dispositions, and patterns of conduct." Stout's argument is helpful because it clarifies that even those who claim the existence of a tradition-free nation-state do indeed work within a tradition. Stout, *Democracy and Tradition*, 3.

Stout goes on to say that these "democratic aspirations" are accompanied by "hatred, cruelty, sloth, envy, greed, and indifference to the suffering of others." He expresses concerns that "new elites" who have come on the scene combined "various forms of vice, bigotry, arrogance, deference, and fear to deform democratic practices" in societies carelessly described as "democratic" (ibid., 9). I cannot tell exactly what Stout means when he says that democratic aspirations are "accompanied by" the vices he names, which seem to be the pursuit of certain "narrow" interests on his view, but surely such things do not

Human Nature, Interest, and Power

To sum up thus far, I am arguing that interests have an inextricably tradition-dependent character. The very intelligibility of an interest requires sequence, and by definition, a sequence arises in a given time, place, and form of life. Interests require stories. But more than this, interests require narratives within larger traditions. The complex relationships of, for example, calculation of advantage, cost-benefit analysis, instrumental reason, or sheer preferences, or even the tautology that "people want what they want," occur in traditions. There is no such thing as interests apart from a form of life. They simply cannot exist prior to a particular history or even apart from (that is, external to) one. Interests are social all the way down. I suspect, finally, that this is a major reason why the concept of interest has taken on its great variability in the history of the West and, for that matter, in the thought of Reinhold Niebuhr.

Seeing interests as tradition-dependent is even more important in the context of international relations. The differences between Western (predominantly American) views of the importance of the separation of church and state as a core political principle and the emergence and resurgence of Islamist forms of government in the Middle East and elsewhere that reject such a separation provide a powerful case in point. In the course of my work and travels, I frequently hear that Iran and Iraq simply need to develop into modern states and to understand and treat religion as the United States does, that is, as individualized, peripheralized, and privatized, a matter of personal belief. If this advice were taken, so the logic goes, then the recalcitrant problems between the United States and these countries would be well on their way to resolution. In the perspective I am offering, such proposals would be naively quaint (if not even laughable) were the issues not so seriously fraught.[17] Descriptions of interest in Iran or Iraq and

---

occur "outside" a democratic tradition. Surely one can argue that such devices are in contradiction to the "democratic aspirations" Stout names, but it is hardly the character of traditions to be without contradiction. I find myself siding here with Anthony Giddens, who cautions that in social analysis, "don't look for the functions social practices fulfill, look for the contradictions they embody!" Giddens, *Central Problems in Social Theory*, 131–64, here 131.

17. In a discussion of secularism, the nation-state, and religion, Asad argues that Islamism's apparent preoccupation with amassing state power is less a symptom of a "commitment to nationalist ideas" and is far more a response to a global situation of compulsive nationalism that sets up the contemporary nation-state as the sole legitimator of identities (whether social or political) and arenas. As he puts it, "No movement that aspires to more than mere belief or inconsequential talk in public can remain indifferent to state power in a secular world." Even when located in a secular order that sees

descriptions of interest in the United States are fundamentally different enterprises, and the ability to conceptualize interest as dependent upon story, and to understand both of these as embedded in powerful traditions, is an utterly indispensable set of skills in today's world.

What is more, the nation-state itself is undergoing major transformations on account of a historically unprecedented process of globalization. A shift in the tradition of the nation-state in the West and a strange new situation in the relationships of the United States to other nations and peoples across the world is part of these transformations. We are also in a time when new traditions may be arising in the networks of a worldwide complex of traditions among peoples, nations, states, regions, and faith traditions. Given this, to work parochially with the notion of interest as it has been expressed, quite variously, within the liberal nation-state in the West is to continue to do grammatical analysis with the promotional literature of the *Titanic*.

Interest, in short, must not be treated as an essentializable concept that is universally understood and operating across the world. Interest is not like some abstract template that we can bring to bear upon the complexities of human motivation in the great variety of forms of life with the expectation that an intelligible insight or explanation will emerge automatically. In a sense, Niebuhr himself recognized this to the extent that he admitted to the reality of "endless variations of interests." However, that this very thin conception of interests simply as "endlessly varied" becomes a tautology seems clear as well. In terms of political analysis, the idea of interest gains analytical traction as it is located *in* the stories of diverse traditions that, together, represent what can be recognized as distinct forms of life. In the important work of political conversation, negotiation, compromise, and agreement, and in ongoing struggle and contention, we are far better served to resist reducing interests to the dynamics of the self compounded in group life so that we can hear the substantive interests people express—seeing interests in the context of the profound sociality of subject-agents, in their stories, and in their traditions that "weave the rich tapestry of the world."[18]

---

itself as "the universal space of the social that sustains the nation-state," Islam cannot on this basis be conflated with nationalism, as if the mere fact of its situation within a nationalist milieu means that Islam automatically and ineluctably becomes nationalist by some bizarre alchemy. Asad notes that though many in the Middle East are convinced that Arab nationalism and Islam are compatible, many others understand such a commitment to be inconsistent. Asad, *FS*, 200.

18. I am indebted to Yvonne Zimmerman for this phrase.

Human Nature, Interest, and Power

POWER

To recap my basic argument concerning power, I have argued that it is a mistake to think of power as something to be possessed. Power flows and circulates. It is exercised tactically and through strategies. Power is the effect of a network of practices—including the practices of discourse. For this reason, understanding power requires attention to the discourses and practices of power that comprise and constitute a form of life. This approach is less susceptible to abstractions that obscure how power actually works in peoples' lives concretely and materially.

Furthermore, I have worked with Foucault's understanding of domination as a corrective to Niebuhr's too exclusive focus on power and the balance of power. Domination, on Foucault's view, cannot be reduced to coercion—though this role should not be ignored—but operates primarily in the forms of normalcy it sustains. Domination functions by means of regimes of truth that powerfully shape what can be said, done, and even thought in a specific form of life. It operates through compelling discourses and through practices that embody its normality. Nevertheless, domination is not a force that operates "above our heads" as something apart from the web of effects that, like any effect, is fed by the energies of bodies, practices, discourses, and relationships with others in forms of life that occupy time and space. In this sense, power—dominative power—is very ordinary and very immanent. The political implications of the concept of domination are extraordinary. For those interested in political engagement, a description of our lives together through a lens of domination opens up for exploration a wide range of questions pertaining to regimes of truth, discourse, practices, and more.

In addition, this perspective raises questions about the "deep grammar" of a form of life—that is, what are the key concepts in use and the relationship of these to one other in the order of domination of a particular time and place?[19] A short example of how "religion" functions and is understood in the United States (as well as several other modern democratic

---

19. Griffiths, "Witness and Conviction in *With the Grain of the Universe*," 70. Griffiths uses the concept of "deep grammar" to suggest the "central semantic terms and their ordinary syntactic relations." Peter Ochs, in a discussion of Hauerwas's *With the Grain of the Universe*, characterizes Wittgenstein's use of "grammar" as "the non-reductive pattern that guides our socio-linguistic practice and offers itself up as the object of our philosophical reflections on the rules of that practice." See Ochs, "On Hauerwas' *With the Grain of the Universe*," 85. Stanley Hauerwas called my attention to these two papers, which are a response to his Gifford Lectures.

Western societies) will clarify what I mean by the relationships among key concepts within any order of domination and the importance of asking critical questions about these concepts and their functional arrangements. In *Genealogies of Religion* Asad traces the history of the concept of religion in the West to the Protestant Reformation, arguing that this was a watershed moment in how religion came to be understood in Western understandings as an individual, private, peripheral matter concerned with beliefs, a matter of personal choice. In and through the Reformation, religion was conceived as a discrete entity with an objectively existing essence—less a set of practices fully integrated into a larger way of life, and more a matter of intellectual assent. As a result, "religion" came to be understood as a "universal transhistorical process"—that is, an overarching genus with specific faith traditions as particular species of this allegedly universal category. Thus began what Asad characterizes as the "theoretical search for an essence of religion."

Asad points out that one of the major upshots of this emergent conception of religion is its conceptual separation from the domain of power.[20] With religion conceived as a universal, objectively existing essence, it was then possible to separate analytically "religion" thus conceived from other domains of power such as politics, law, and science. It is this kind of separation of varieties of power (including but by no means limited to "religion") into discrete domains that, Asad argues, characterize social and political arrangements as distinctively modern in form so that the processes through which religion came to be understood as its own discrete essence—that is, *not* politics, *not* science, *not* law—actually converge with the larger processes of modernity *itself* that so permeate and organize our lives. Indeed, what Asad calls the "separation of religion from power" is the dominant formation of power that permeates and characterizes established forms of life in the United States. The deep grammar of this arrangement of power is pervasive, shaping the lives not only of those who identify as "religious" according to its terms, but even the lives of those who do not. While there are discourses, practices, and forms of life that challenge the deep grammar of this power formation, they are not established orders commensurate with that of the dominant understanding of "religion." Thus they are sites of resistance to a much larger normalcy.

---

20. Asad, *GR*, 28f. In this discussion Asad identifies historical moves that led to this concept of religion as a transhistorical essence and uses these in a critique of anthropologist Clifford Geertz, 29–54. See also Scott and Hirschkind, *PSM*, 287f.

Human Nature, Interest, and Power

As a person shaped by an understanding of the church as a community of faith that is called to be in some tension with the world in which it is situated and to provide an alternative to that world, I find Foucault's understanding of domination immensely helpful for understanding the contemporary situation of the church in relation to the state in the context of the United States. Currently, the state is invested in maintaining a separation between public and private spheres of life, and a chief strategy in creating and maintaining this separation is to expel religion and individuals' faith traditions from the public sphere and relegate them to the private and personal sphere of life. Foucault's analysis highlights that the immense amount of energy that the state devotes to creating and policing this separation is a display of power. What this situation also means, moreover, is that there is a significant sense in which the fundamental character of the church is determined by an external authority. Such a situation raises critical ethical and ecclesiological questions, and it seems to me that this domination ought to be carefully discerned and countered in both the discourse and the practices of the church.

Yet such discernment and resistance to the operation of state power in shaping the church's form and function in contemporary American life face difficult odds because these require people of faith to question and rethink the way they understand religion at a very fundamental level. Put another way, this is difficult work precisely because the dominance of this understanding of religion is so pervasive that most American Christians not only hold it themselves, but deeply believe it to be true. To challenge the domination of this formation of power requires an alternative formation of religious sensibilities. Thus a politics of resistance requires a politics of formation.

If a politics of resistance requires an alternative politics of formation, how is such a politics of formation embraced and enacted? Asad suggests attention to "authorizing discourse," a concept we developed in chapter 5, which Asad understands as a form of internal power where people engage in practices of formation in making and remaking themselves. An authorizing discourse moves in multiple directions at the same time. It offers the possibility of resistance to secular powers and the nation-state and, most importantly, opens up space for alternative discourses and practices necessary to form subject-agents of another order. In other words, it is through authorizing discourse that the normalizing and dominative powers of the nation-state can be resisted and that other possibilities can open up. Faith traditions of various forms have the potential to interrupt the state-based formation of subject-agents as secular citizens whose religious commitments are only private. Faith traditions that seek an embodied faith not reducible to beliefs are a resource through which to learn the skills and capacities to be able to refuse the relegation of religion to the private, the peripheral, and the personal.[21]

With regard to power, it can no longer be seen as a possession; it does not reside at the apex of some imaginary pyramid. Understood as the effects of a network of practices—including the practices of discourse—power takes on the character of flows, of trajectories, and of strategies, as we have seen. Furthermore, in these terms an analysis of power will attend to the discourses and practices of power in a form of life. Such approaches will help us avoid the use of abstractions that obscure these more concrete and material moves of power as it courses through the effects of strategic relations in a form of life.

During the years 1967 to 1973, I conducted a longitudinal study of power in the city of Kansas City, Missouri, with the help of more than a hundred students. Much of the work took place in a course on community power and the church that I taught annually at the time. The first part of this study was a probe of the business community that compiled a list of the top CEOs and largest corporations in the city. Students put together brief histories of these corporations and biographies of their CEOs. Second, we interviewed half of the political ward committeemen and women of the city, asking them whom they saw as the most influential people there. Third, we also studied four of the major issues that Kansas City faced then: the building of a mid-city freeway, the construction of a twin professional sports stadium complex, the development and building of a university medical school, and a city redevelopment proposal by an

---

21. To clarify, I am not claiming that in order for the church to stand as a legitimate alternative to the hegemony of the market and the state it must be completely extricated from them. To posit the church as representing some type of pure and pristine alternative is simply disingenuous, as evidenced by its hungry ambition and greedy pursuit of power and wealth; by revelations of sexual violence perpetrated by clergy; by ecclesial accommodation of an idolatrous patriotism; by the support it has lent to the nation-state in the pursuit of war in myriad times and places; by its capitulation to the "entrepreneurial spirit" in its search for leadership models borrowed from corporate America; and by its capacity to turn inward and ignore the poor, the widow, and the orphan. The church is not exempted from or untainted by the dynamics of power in which it is situated. Nevertheless, it is called to a fundamentally different logic of power, that of a response to divine love.

insurance company that would have taken land, through eminent domain, in a sizable and stable residential area. We pulled together chronologies of the development of each of these issues and compiled lists and biographies of the key business, professional, and political people who were involved in making the decisions about these issues, and then interviewed as many of these constituents as possible. We also examined those holding offices in the economic, political, and social institutions in the city that were strategic to each of these projects. In addition, we asked people involved in the four issues whom they regarded as the most influential individuals on that issue. Finally, we identified which individuals were on which side in each of these issues and drew conclusions as to who had power based ultimately on who prevailed in how a project proceeded and was carried out.

We found no power elite; we found no conspiracies that determined the direction and the final decision on these issues. There was no oligopoly, at least not over the city as a whole. What we found instead was a power structure that we characterized as "highly pluralistic" when not "fractionated"—meaning that there were instances when decisions could not be made because power was so dispersed. As one highly esteemed mayor described Kansas City in an interview, "we are a loose, tribal democracy."

Having received a small grant for this research from a church agency, I drafted a report on the study in 1975 but never attempted formally to publish the findings for the simple reason that, at the time, I did not believe they were sufficiently significant to warrant publication.

I recently reread this report and I came away wishing I had known Foucault's work at that time. His attention to discourse and practices would have made the report not only more concrete and focused, but with his methodology of an ascending analysis of power, we could have identified and named practices, relationships, and effects that the analytic categories and framework we had at our disposal (such as "a plural power structure" and the highly abstract concept of "fractionated") obscured. Our language and categories prevented us from doing the kind of penetrating analysis we desired. It is not as if the report was not helpful at all. I used it in lectures, in consultations with community organizing efforts in the city, and in actions around other issues that surfaced in subsequent years. Now, however, I am painfully aware of how much more useful that work could have been had it been informed in a more thoroughgoing sense by Foucault's understanding of power.

Political Implications

As I said earlier, I am currently active in broad-based organizing in Phoenix, Arizona. One aspect of this work is what we call "research actions," which basically involve interviewing key individuals actively engaged with important issues before the community. The purpose of these interviews is to discern what is happening and to identify power relationships. While it is helpful to learn from interviewees the names of others whom they regard as significantly involved in particular issues, I have found that what is far more helpful is when interviewees are able to report and describe the specific discourses and practices of power that accrue around an issue. So, for instance, we recently tried to get a conversation with a significant state agency and ran into resistance. In our conversations with other state figures, however, we found out that the board of that agency is dissatisfied with the work of the staff, which attempts to run the board. We have learned of revealing comments and moves by board members that open a number of avenues for us to pursue. When the discussion moves to this level of describing actual discursive and nondiscursive practices, the concrete, material flows, trajectories, and strategies of power are clarified and revealed in ways that mere lists of people and summaries of their various positions in the community, their reputations for power, and their engagements and "wins," no matter how carefully crafted, can never fully communicate. Who attended a meeting and who spoke there may indicate a basic framework of power, but such a framework is no substitute for learning of gatherings before or after the meeting and what happened at them, or of the discourses that proved compelling before, during, and after the meeting. This is a more intricate power analysis that, beyond comprehending the framework of power in a particular location on a specific issue, gets at the fine *texture* of how power moves and operates.

A political implication of these insights is the need to focus on the discourses and practices of power, an effort that can be neglected when essentialized concepts like the will to power or the existential dynamics of the self arrogantly in pursuit of self-interests are emphasized. An analysis of power is far better served by asking questions about what is going on at this material level of discourses and practices than it is by presuming that certain dynamics of the self have already determined the agenda. Furthermore, placing analytical energy on learning to know the discourses and to recognize the practices of power within a form of life opens the possibility for comprehending a greater complexity of and fine gradations in power and how it operates within a community that is more rich and relationally nuanced than analyses concentrated exclusively on discrete individuals and their pursuit of self-interest, whether individually or in group life. Focusing on the discourses and the practices in an ascending analysis of power not only makes possible a far more nuanced understanding of how power operates in a particular time and place, but it also opens up a plethora of opportunities to engage power, to modify its practices, to change relationships, and to shift its ascent in these basic forms and expressions.

Now, by saying that change is possible, I do not mean that any of this is easily accomplished. Max Weber once said that "politics is a strong and slow boring of hard boards."[22] The last decade of community organizing has instructed me again that influencing the flows of power is incredibly demanding. It requires seemingly endless conversations with a wide variety of people; the utter necessity of listening to people; initiating and developing ongoing relationships with them; building trust; getting people together to share their stories and to work at finding common interests and, within these, common good; and the continual going back to rebuild connections with people. It also involves cultivating the ability to shift perspective, responses, and priorities as situations change; developing the skills to be able to work in these ways, including an ability to take on infinite "scut work," such as the mundane tasks of paying attention to details, doing the little things, making the phone calls, writing the notes of appreciation and gratitude, and remembering to touch base with people; and a sheer doggedness to stay at it.[23] These are only a few of the things that constitute my understanding of the "boring of hard boards."[24]

A second implication is the importance of working locally. With the ascending analysis of power one begins to understand that any great social change is typically the result of long, hard local effort. The civil rights movement is a powerful case in point. Utterly essential to this movement was the ongoing, down-on-the-ground organizing of African Americans and their allies at the grassroots level. It is not my intent to detract from the leadership and oratory of Martin Luther King Jr., which was, indeed, extraordinary. My point is that King's emergence as a powerful, charismatic

22. Weber, "Politics as a Vocation," 128.

23. I get this phrase from Lena DiCicco, a social worker in Boston back in the mid-1960s. In the dictionary one of the meanings of the word *scut* is a contemptible person. When DiCicco used the phrase "scut work," she used it to mean lowly tasks or simply the less exciting, ongoing routine of the kind I describe above.

24. In this connection see the extraordinary chapter on organizing in Payne, *I've Got the Light of Freedom*, 236–64.

leader who could unify the movement and elevate it to the national stage was the direct result of many years and literally countless hours of the very difficult work of organizing African Americans and their white allies at the grassroots level. Without this invisible work, the civil rights movement would never have had—*could* not have had—the success it did.[25]

An analysis of power that focuses on discourse and practices also has implications for national or international relations. The Watergate fiasco in the early 1970s threw into stark relief the extent to which power is not a possession that an individual or group of individuals "has." The cover-up by the Nixon administration, the actions of Nixon and his national staff, including the abuse of office of the presidency, reveal the extent to which power is, instead, a mass of strategic relations exercised in and through a wide range of practices that, taken alone, may seem rather disconnected from "Power" writ large. Carl Bernstein and Bob Woodward's *All the President's Men* details a riveting account of these days in the Nixon White House. Reading their book as a display of discourses and practices provides an illuminating description. Understood like this, we can see how in the Watergate situation the White House itself represented a discrete locality and how, as the nation and the world witnessed, it is possible for the man in the most powerful position on earth to be drummed from office.

The Lyndon B. Johnson presidential administration also poignantly exemplifies this conception of what power is and how it operates. Johnson was among the legislative and political geniuses of the twentieth century, but his misguided handling of the Vietnam War will almost certainly be remembered as one of the most serious critiques of his presidency. The flows of power between Johnson, McNamara, the Department of Defense, the Joint Chiefs of the Staff, and the Congress compose a virtual Greek tragedy of a seemingly inevitable descent into disaster and failure. The miscommunication and the stalemate between McNamara and the Joint Chiefs of Staff; Johnson's attempt to underplay the Vietnam War until after his 1964 reelection; and the failure of the Joint Chiefs of Staff to heed all of the warnings evidently on display, as documented by H. R. McMaster in *Dereliction of Duty*, are only a few of the complex interactions that led to the calamity that was Vietnam.[26]

---

25. Similar things could be said about the women's movement, the labor movement, and, for that matter, prohibition.

26. McMaster, *Dereliction of Duty*. This book includes transcripts of meetings, messages, memos, and reports that trace the developments of this period of the Johnson administration and its pursuit of the war. For extraordinary studies of the political career

Human Nature, Interest, and Power

A more recent example is the response of the Bush administration to the terrorist attacks of September 11, 2001, on the World Trade Center and the Pentagon. Without careful attention to how the president and administration officials framed their public remarks to the nation immediately following the attacks and in subsequent days, and lacking sufficient knowledge of the consultations, meetings, ideas, and conceptual frameworks that informed and shaped how the administration understood and discursively framed the events and their aftermath in those terrible days, it is simply impossible to understand why the decision was made to attack Iraq since there was no actual evidence of Iraq's having or using weapons of mass destruction and, even more immediately to the point, of any relationship between the events of 9/11 and the Iraqi government. Without attention to the role of discourse, the U.S. response is utterly incomprehensible. Yet these are the things of which so much of politics is constituted. When policy and decisions move up ladders of high abstraction to talk about "protecting the free world" or declaring a "war on terrorism," it is difficult to see and focus on the capillaries of power at work in a national administration and relationships between these capillaries of power and the Congress, the military, the media, lobbyists, etc. All of these relationships are instances of flows of power.

As I argued in chapter 4, Niebuhr's privileged concept of the "balance of power" cannot possibly describe the complexities of power either within nations or between them. The concept is not sophisticated enough to convey the complex flows, strategic relations, and relational complexities that comprise normal, everyday national and international affairs. As Michael Sheehan observes, the balance of power concept is often used ideologically to justify political decisions that are actually made for quite different reasons that cannot be publicly legitimated. In short, a concept such as "balance of power" is as relative as the dynamics it seeks to describe.

At the same time, it goes without saying that power also works to oppress, exploit, perpetrate violence against, and abase those who are relatively powerless. While I question the metaphors of balance/imbalance as a way to characterize the way power works, especially in our contemporary setting, I do not want to ignore or underestimate the capacity of those who

---

of Lyndon B. Johnson, see the four volumes of Robert A. Caro: *The Path to Power; Means of Ascent; Master of the Senate*; and *The Passage of Power*. These are virtual catalogs of the discourses and practices of the Congress during Johnson's political career.

inhabit strategic positions and relationships to use power for dehumanizing ends.

The twentieth century, the bloodiest in history, has only just passed. Abuses of power stand through the decades of that century like tombs in a graveyard, and the first decade of the twenty-first century does not indicate a new time of peace. So the astute reader may well wonder how I reconcile this observation with what we see as the most morally and politically substantive implications of the argument I have developed over the course of these pages—namely, the contention that massive differences in power notwithstanding, no one is ever completely powerless. This bears repeating: no one is ever *completely* powerless.

More than that, established power is ever composed of the flows, trajectories, and strategic relations that are integral to the form of life in which they are situated. Power is built in an ascending manner, from the bottom up, and constituted by a mammoth range of practices. Power draws legitimation from regimes of truth, or from what is able in a particular time and place to pass as "true," and it operates in and through the frames of normalcy of everyday life. Nonetheless, power is not permanent. The energies, relations, discourses, and practices of power are ever contingent. Power has a historicity. Arrangements of power in a time and place finally end. The sanctions of that power arrangement finally pass on. Even people in powerful positions die and their connections dissolve. Nations rise and fall, and, as scripture says, "the nations are like a drop from a bucket" (Isa 40:15a).

Yet the sure knowledge that no nation or regime is permanent is scant solace to a single mother with children who faces the grinding reality of poverty, to the peasants of the world, to working people who are underpaid and face unending debt, to those who live under totalitarian regimes, to those whose lives are ripped apart by war, to those who die as "collateral damage" from so-called smart weapons, to those who are victimized by and then blamed for racism, and many others. To people such as these the contingency and historicity of power is hardly the harbinger of a new day. In fact, Foucault's conception of power and history is not premised on modernity's master narrative of progress. Contra the narrative of progress, Foucault reveals that instead we go from one formation of power to the next—"from domination to domination," as he says.[27] We go from the formation of one normality to another, from the combined logics and the sub-

---

27. Foucault, *FR*, 85.

jectivations of one order to another, each with its own coercion, violence, and corruption.

As tragic as that can be, the relations and flows of power do not remain the same. As it was for the peasants in the Rangpur District rebellion (see chapter 6), where neither the landholders nor the government controlled the final outcomes in that time and place, so it is today for us. Even though the landholders and the colonial government were more powerfully positioned than the peasants, the peasants' actions were not inconsequential to the outcome of that conflict. They were not utterly powerless. Despite attempts at strategy, uses of language to contain and control the conflict, rules and regulations propagated to quash it, and the elaborate efforts expended to manage it, the landholders and the government still were not able to maintain the status quo they sought to preserve. In the end, albeit in a much longer time frame than the peasants ever envisioned, things shifted and, slowly, change came that benefited them. Of course, events do not always or inevitably work this way. But my point is that power is not absolute. It is a *relation* of effects, and its movement is like a flow. The relations and flows of power are not the holdings of any establishment, and concepts such as the balance of power are as relative as the dynamics they seek to describe.

CONCLUSION

Briefly, let me draw a few conclusions. First, in this essay I oppose Niebuhr's concept of a universal, primordial self and challenge the binary conceptualities that reduce and obscure the far more complex dynamics of a constituted subject formed in the discourses, practices, and specific structures of life in a given time and place. I reject attempts to bring so-called universal concepts to subject-agents and call for a heightened sense of the otherness of those in different forms of life. With Niebuhr I challenge the notion of the free autonomous self but move beyond him to pose an understanding of freedom as capaciousness, as the capacity to work in the range of practices, skills, and tacit subtleties of a form of life.

Second, I demonstrate that interest or self-interest is not some essential concept universally understood and functioning in the same way around the world. It is not some abstract template to be placed upon the complex introspective practices and motivations of subject-agents in the wide range of linguistic, sociocultural, and historical textures of the world that will remain neither still nor yield to such easy generalization. I offer instead an understanding of interests in their rich sociality as embedded in stories that are tradition-dependent.

Third, I challenge the notion of power as something to be possessed. Rather, it is constituted of the effects of a network of practices of a discursive as well as a nondiscursive kind. To understand power is to perform an ascending analysis of the relational effects of the discourses and practices that encompass a form of life. This approach to power has rich implications for national and international relations with its capacity to characterize the complicated flows, strategic relations, and multilevel dealings that make up the ongoing, day in and day out events of national and international affairs. Furthermore, Sheehan's historical study demonstrates the great variability of the concept of the balance of power in its use, its employment for ideological purposes, and—even in its Hobbesian and Grotian forms—its highly abstract character that begs for concrete display in a given time and place. Also, I offer Foucault's understanding of domination as a corrective to Niebuhr's overemphasis on the balance of power. Foucault's concept of domination is a far more pervasive notion functioning mainly in terms of normalcy. While coercion and violence are not absent from this notion, it refers in a far more encompassing way to the ordinary, to what is typical and conventional in a form of life.

Finally, a central application of the reconceptions of human nature, interest, and power that I have proposed is that of the crucial importance of what we do in the formation of ourselves—that is, of the significance of tradition in disciplined discourse and faithful practice. As I have argued, no one is ever completely powerless. Tradition, discourse, and faithful practice thus emerge as potential resources that can be utilized for communities to come together to challenge the dominations, the normalcies, and the coercions of our times.

Bibliography

Allen, Danielle. *Talking to Strangers: Anxieties of Citizenship since Brown v. Board of Education*. Chicago: University of Chicago Press, 2004.
Arendt, Hannah. *The Human Condition*. 2nd ed. Chicago: University of Chicago Press, 1998.
Asad, Talal. *Formations of the Secular: Christianity, Islam, Modernity*. Stanford: Stanford University Press, 2003.
———. *Genealogies of Religion: Discipline and Reasons of Power in Christianity and Islam*. Baltimore: Johns Hopkins University Press, 1993.
———. "Responses." In *Powers of the Secular Modern: Talal Asad and His Interlocutors*, edited by David Scott and Charles Hirschkind, 206–41. Stanford: Stanford University Press, 2006.
———. "The Trouble of Thinking: An Interview with Talal Asad." In *Powers of the Secular Modern: Talal Asad and His Interlocutors*, edited by David Scott and Charles Hirschkind, 243–303. Stanford: Stanford University Press, 2006.
Bell, Daniel, Jr. *Liberation Theology at the End of History: The Refusal to Cease Suffering*. London: Routledge, 2001.
Benne, Robert. *Ordinary Saints: An Introduction to the Christian Life*. Minneapolis: Fortress, 2003.
Bernstein, Carl, and Bob Woodward. *All the President's Men*. New York: Simon & Schuster, 1974.
Best, Steven, and Douglas Kellner. *Postmodern Theory: Critical Interrogations*. New York: Guilford, 1991.
Blyth, Mark. *Great Transformations: Economic Ideas and Institutional Change in the Twentieth Century*. Cambridge: Cambridge University Press, 2002.
Bobbitt, Philip. *The Shield of Achilles: War, Peace, and the Course of History*. New York: Anchor, 2002.
Brown, Robert McAfee, editor. *The Essential Reinhold Niebuhr: Selected Essays and Addresses*. New Haven: Yale University Press, 1986.
Brunner, Emil. *Man in Revolt: A Christian Anthropology*. Translated by Olive Wyon. London: R.T.S.-Lutterworth, 1939.
Caro, Robert A. *Master of the Senate*. The Years of Lyndon Johnson 3. New York: Vintage, 2003.
———. *Means of Ascent*. The Years of Lyndon Johnson 2. New York: Vintage, 1991.
———. *The Passage of Power: The Years of Lyndon Johnson* 4. New York: Vintage, 2012.
———. *The Path to Power*. The Years of Lyndon Johnson 1. New York: Vintage, 1990.
Connolly, William E. *Capitalism and Christianity, American Style*. Durham: Duke University Press, 2008.
———. *Why I Am Not a Secularist*. Minneapolis: University of Minnesota Press, 1999.

Bibliography

Crouter, Richard. *Reinhold Niebuhr: On Politics, Religion, and Christian Faith*. Oxford: Oxford University Press, 2010.

Edwards, James C. *Ethics Without Philosophy: Wittgenstein and the Moral Life*. Gainesville: University Press of Florida, 1985.

Foucault, Michel. *Discipline and Punishment: The Birth of the Prison*. New York: Vintage, 1977.

———. *The Foucault Reader*. Edited by Paul Rabinow. New York: Pantheon, 1984.

———. *The Order of Things: An Archaeology of the Human Sciences*. New York: Vintage, 1970.

———. *Power/Knowledge: Selected Interviews and Other Writings, 1972–1977*. Edited by Colin Gordon. New York: Pantheon, 1977.

———. "Two Lectures." In *Critique and Power: Recasting the Foucault/Habermas Debate*, edited by Michael Kelly, 17–46. Cambridge: MIT Press, 1994.

Fox, Richard Wightman. *Reinhold Niebuhr: A Biography*. New York: Pantheon, 1985.

Giddens, Anthony. *Central Problems in Social Theory: Action, Structure, and Contradiction in Social Theory*. Berkeley: University of California Press, 1979.

Gilkey, Langdon. *On Niebuhr: A Theological Study*. Chicago: University of Chicago Press, 2001.

Griffiths, Paul. "Witness and Conviction in *With the Grain of the Universe*." *Modern Theology* 19 (2003) 67–75.

Gulick, E. V. *Europe's Classical Balance of Power*. Ithaca: Cornell University Press, 1955.

Harrison, Beverly. *Making the Connections: Essays in Feminist Social Ethics*. Edited by Carol S. Robb. Boston: Beacon, 1985.

Hauerwas, Stanley J. *Performing the Faith: Bonhoeffer and the Practice of Nonviolence*. Grand Rapids: Brazos, 2004.

———. *With the Grain of the Universe: The Church's Witness and Natural Theology*. Grand Rapids: Brazos, 2001.

Hirschman, Albert O. *The Passions and the Interests: Political Arguments for Capitalism before Its Triumph*. Princeton: Princeton University Press, 1977.

———. *Rival Views of Market Society and Other Recent Essays*. Cambridge: Harvard University Press, 1992.

Holmes, Stephen. *Passions and Constraint: On the Theory of Liberal Democracy*. Chicago: University of Chicago Press, 1995.

Kegley, Charles W., and Robert W. Bretall, editors. *Reinhold Niebuhr: His Religious, Social, and Political Thought*. New York: Macmillan, 1961.

LeDoux, Joseph. *The Emotional Brain: The Mysterious Underpinnings of Emotional Life*. New York: Simon & Schuster, 1996.

Lovin, Robin W. *Christian Realism and the New Realities*. Cambridge: Cambridge University Press, 2008.

———. *Reinhold Niebuhr and Christian Realism*. Cambridge: Cambridge University Press, 1995.

MacIntyre, Alasdair C. *After Virtue: A Study in Moral Theory*. 2nd ed. Notre Dame: University of Notre Dame Press, 1984.

———. *The MacIntyre Reader*. Edited by Kelvin Knight. Notre Dame: University of Notre Dame Press, 1998.

———. *Three Rival Versions of Moral Enquiry: Encyclopedia, Genealogy, and Tradition*. Notre Dame: University of Notre Dame Press, 1990.

———. *Whose Justice? Which Rationality?* Notre Dame: University of Notre Dame Press, 1988.

Mahmood, Saba. *Politics of Piety: The Islamic Revival and the Feminist Subject.* Princeton: Princeton University Press, 2005.

Mauss, Marcel. *The Gift: Forms and Functions of Exchange in Archaic Societies.* Translated by W. D. Halls. London: Routledge Classics, 2002.

McMaster, H. R. *Dereliction of Duty: Johnson, McNamara, the Joint Chiefs of Staff, and the Lies that Led to Vietnam.* New York: HarperPerennial, 1998.

Morgenthau, Hans J. *Politics Among Nations: The Struggle for Power and Peace.* 5th ed. New York: Knopf, 1978.

Murdoch, Iris. *The Sovereignty of the Good.* London: Routledge & Kegan Paul, 1970.

Niebuhr, Reinhold. "Augustine's Political Realism." In *Christian Realism and Political Problems*, 119–46. New York: Scribner's, 1953.

———. *The Children of Light and the Children of Darkness: A Vindication of Democracy and a Critique of Its Traditional Defense.* New York: Scribner's, 1944.

———. *Christian Realism and Political Problems.* New York: Scribner's, 1953.

———. *Christianity and Power Politics.* New York: Scribner's, 1940.

———. *Essays in Applied Christianity.* Selected and edited by D. B. Robertson. New York: Living Age, 1959.

———. *Faith and History: A Comparison of Christian and Modern Views of History.* New York: Scribner's, 1949.

———. *Faith and Politics.* Edited by Ronald Stone. New York: G. Braziller, 1968.

———. *Man's Nature and His Communities: Essays on the Dynamics and Enigmas of Man's Personal and Social Existence.* New York: Scribner's, 1965.

———. *Moral Man and Immoral Society: A Study in Ethics and Politics.* New York: Scribner's, 1932.

———. *The Nature and Destiny of Man: A Christian Interpretation.* 2 vols. New York: Scribner's, 1941–43.

———. "Power and Justice." *Christianity and Society* 8 (1942) 9–10.

———. *Reinhold Niebuhr: Theologian of Public Life.* Edited by Larry Rasmussen. Minneapolis: Fortress, 1988.

———. *The Self and the Dramas of History.* New York: Scribner's, 1955.

———. *The Structure of Nations and Empires.* New York: Scribner's, 1959.

Nietzsche, Friedrich W. *Toward a Genealogy of Morals.* In *Basic Writings of Nietzsche*, edited and translated by Walter Kaufmann, 450–54. New York: Viking, 1954.

Ochs, Peter. "On Hauerwas' *With the Grain of the Universe.*" *Modern Theology* 19 (2003) 77–88.

O'Donovan, Oliver. *The Ways of Judgment.* Grand Rapids: Eerdmans, 2005.

Ong, Walter J. *Orality and Literacy: The Technologizing of the Word.* New York: Routledge, 1982.

———. *The Presence of the Word: Some Prolegomena for Cultural and Religious History.* New Haven: Yale University Press, 1967.

Payne, Charles M. *I've Got the Light of Freedom: The Organizing Tradition and the Mississippi Freedom Struggle.* Berkeley: University of California Press, 1995.

Posen, Barry. *The Sources of Military Doctrine: France, Britain and Germany between the World Wars.* Ithaca: Cornell University Press, 1984.

Schroeder, Paul W. "The Nineteenth-Century System: Balance of Power or Political Equilibrium?" *Review of International Studies* 15 (1989) 135–53.

———. "The Neo-Realist Theory of International Politics: An Historian's View." Occasional paper, Program in Arms Control, Disarmament and Internation Security, University of Illinois at Urbana-Champaign, 1991.

Bibliography

Scott, David. "The Tragic Sensibility of Talal Asad." In *Powers of the Secular Modern*, edited by David Scott and Charles Hirschkind, 134–53. Stanford: Stanford University Press, 2006.

Scott, David, and Charles Hirschkind, editors. *Powers of the Secular Modern: Talal Asad and His Interlocutors*. Stanford: Stanford University Press, 2006.

Sennett, Richard, and Jonathan Cobb. *The Hidden Injuries of Class*. New York: Norton, 1972.

Sheehan, Michael. *The Balance of Power: History and Theory*. London: Routledge, 1996.

Smith, Adam. *An Inquiry into the Nature and Causes of the Wealth of Nations*. Edited by Edwin Cannan. New York: Modern Library, 1937.

Stone, Ronald H. *Christian Realism and Peacemaking: Issues in U.S. Foreign Policy*. Nashville: Abingdon, 1988.

———. *Prophetic Realism: Beyond Militarism and Pacifism in an Age of Terror*. Nashville: Abingdon, 1988.

———. *Reinhold Niebuhr: Prophet to Politicians*. Nashville: Abingdon, 1972.

Stout, Jeffrey. *Blessed Are the Organized: Grassroots Democracy in America*. Princeton: Princeton University Press, 2010.

———. *Democracy and Tradition*. Princeton: Princeton University Press, 2004.

Weber, Max. "Politics as a Vocation." In *From Max Weber: Essays in Sociology*, translated and edited by C. Wright Mills and H. H. Gerth, 77–128. Routledge Classics in Sociology. New York: Routledge, 2009.

Wilson, Jon E. "Subjects and Agents in the History of Imperialism and Resistance." In *Powers of the Secular Modern*, edited by David Scott and Charles Hirschkind, 180–205. Stanford: Stanford University Press, 2006.

Wolf, William John. "Reinhold Niebuhr's Doctrine of Man." In *Reinhold Niebuhr: His Religious, Social, and Political Thought*, edited by Charles W. Kegley and Robert W. Bretall, 229–49. New York: Macmillan, 1961.

Wolin, Sheldon. *Politics and Vision: Continuity and Innovation in Western Political Thought*. Princeton: Princeton University Press, 2006.

Index

agency, 10, 13f., 24f., 32, 81f., 114, 127f., 127f.n11, 138, 154f.
Allen, Danielle, 141, 141n10, 163
anxiety, 3, 20, 26–28, 31f., 39, 43
Arendt, Hannah, 140, 140n7, 143f., 163
Asad, Talal, x, xv, xvi, 9n22, 9n11, 24, 24n53, 24–26, 29n61, 32n71, 76n24, 77n28, 112–14, 117, 127f., 130, 147n17, 151n20, 163
Augustine, 1, 20–22, 45, 54
authorizing discourse, 112–14, 138, 152

Bell, Daniel, Jr., 139, 139n5, 163
Benne, Robert, 105n44, 163
Best, Steven, 79n36, 163
Blyth, Mark, 64–66, 163
Bobbitt, Philip, 107–8, 107n49, 134, 163
body, embodiment, 11–12, 17, 25f., 31, 78n29, 79, 81f., 113, 128
brain research, 31f., 31n69
broad-based organizing, 10, 13, 141, 144f., 154–57, 156n24, 165
Brown, Robert McAfee, xv, 43n30, 163
Brunner, Emil, 1, 1n1, 163
Bush, George W., 158

Caro, Robert A., 158n26, 163
church, 111–35, 111n1, 153n21
concepts, 8n18, 10, 18, 20, 25–27, 29–30, 34f., 48, 53, 59, 65–67, 68, 83, 101, 102, 128, 130, 132, 134–35, 136f., 151, 155, 160
Connolly, William E., xv, xvi, 30–33, 61–66, 142, 163
Crouter, Richard, 164

David, King, of Israel, 146f.
definitions, problems with, 10f., 34, 52, 61, 75, 83, 129
discourse, 8–9n18, 11, 23n51, 30, 79, 79n34–36, 82, 84, 94, 101, 103, 105, 106, 112–14, 113f.n11, 124, 138, 146, 150, 152f., 154, 157f., 161

Edwards, James C., 137, 137nn2–3, 164

formation, 7–8, 8n18, 10, 13, 16, 19, 25, 30, 80, 111–18
Foucault, Michel, xv, xvi, 8n18, 9, 10–13, 76–79, 79–81, 101, 107, 113n8, 132, 132n19, 133n20, 134, 136, 136n1, 159, 159n26, 159n27, 164, versus Niebuhr, 81–84, 109
Fox, Richard Wightman, 164
freedom, 2–5, 5f., 6n15, 9–15, 16, 24, 26, 27, 38, 45f., 69, 72, 81, 115, 128, 134, 138–40, 160

Giddens, Anthony, 148n16, 164
Gilkey, Langdon, xvi, 21n44, 117, 164

Index

Graham, Billy, 115
Griffiths, Paul, 150n19, 164
Gulick, E. V., 96n26, 164

habitus, 25–27, 112–14, 128, 140
Hadot, Pierre, 9
Hauerwas, Stanley J., x, xiii, 143n12, 145, 145n14, 150n19, 164
Hirschman, Albert O., xvi, 53–61, 65, 164
Hirschkind, Charles, xvi, 151n20, 163, 166
historical contingency, 18
Holmes, Stephen, 54n55, 58n73, 164
human nature, ix, x, xi, 1–33, 38, 47, 67, 68–69, 73, 85, 102, 111n1, 119, 121f., 127–29, 134–40, 161. *See also* self

Individualism, 17f., 23, 115
Individuality, 16–20, 135
interest, self-interest, xi, 10, 25, 34–67, 124, 126; analogies of interest as continuum, as bush, 141–42; as tradition dependent, 140–49, 160f.; Connolly on interest, 61–65, 66f., 131f.n18; Hirschman on history of concept of interest, 53–61, 66f.; Niebuhr's use of, 35–53, 66f., 68, 74, 83, 85, 86, 102, 103, 119, 120–22, 128, 129–32, 134f.; story and interest, 143–46
introspection, practices of, 20, 24, 26–30, 33, 83, 127, 128, 137

Johnson, Lyndon Baines, 157, 157f.n26, 163, 165

Kansas City power, 153f.
Kegley, Charles W., and Robert W. Bretall, xvi, 1n1, 34n4, 164
Kellner, Douglas, 79n36, 163

King, Martin Luther, Jr., 156

ladder of abstraction, the, xi, 26
Ledoux, Joseph, 31, 164
Litchfield, Randy, xiii
Lovin, Robin W., xv, xvi, 34, 35, 36, 36n8, 42, 52, 53, 104–8, 134, 164
Lowry, Gene, 9–10

MacIntyre, Alasdair C., x, 113, 113n8, 143, 143n12, 145n14, 145n15, 147, 164
Mahmood, Saba, x, xvi, 7–15, 24, 28f., 127f., 134, 165
majesty of the state, of government, 83, 87, 87n6, 92n17
Mauss, Marcel, 25, 30, 165
McMaster, H. R., 157, 157n26, 165
meaning, 3, 5, 8n18, 9, 9n22, 53, 117, 146
Methodist School of Theology in Ohio, xviii
modern era, world, society, culture, state, 4, 7, 14, 17, 18, 19, 39, 48, 70f., 72n16, 82, 87, 88, 91, 93, 105, 134, 148, 150f
Morgenthau, Hans J., 165
Mosque women's movement, Cairo, 7, 10, 13, 28f.
Murdoch, Iris, 138n4, 165

Nietzsche, Friedrich W., 61, 165
Nixon, Richard M., 157

Ochs, Peter, 150n19, 165
O'Donovan, Oliver, 20–24, 83
Ong, Walter J., 29f., 165

Payne, Charles M., 156n24, 165
Posen, Barry, 99n34, 165
power, as a relation of force, 10–11, 76, 81; as formation, 10, 13, 80f., 151, 111–18; 151–53,

Index

159, 161; as productive, 10–12, 81, 109; ascending analysis of, 77f., 80, 83f., 107, 109, 154–56, 161; balance, equilibrium, of power, x, 68, 85–110, 126, 136, 150, 158, 160, 161; critique of Niebuhr's concept of power, x, 68–84, 88, 94, 102; critique of Niebuhr's concept of balance of power, 94–104; discourses/practices of, 12, 15, 78, 107, 109f., 134, 135, 150, 153, 155, 157, 157f.n26, 159, 161; economic power, 16, 70f., 87, 93; Foucault on, 10f., 10n23, 12, 13, 76–79, 81–84, 101f., 107, 109, 132f., 133n21–22, 134, 159f.; internal power, 111–18, 133, 152; macro/micro power, 12, 76–79, 80f., 83–84, 103, 106f., 109, 134; Niebuhr's concept of, 68–73; power/truth, 8f.n18, 79–80, 84; Sheehan on, 94–104, 158, 166; strategic relations of force, 78, 132, 153, 157–159, 161; types of, 69–71, 75, 106f.; will to power, 73–75

Rangpur revolt, 119–35, 142f., 160
Rasmussen, Larry, xin1, xiii, xvi, 34, 35n5, 52, 111n1, 165
realism, political, 33, 34–37, 44f., 47, 49, 51f., 104–7, 111n1, 121f., 128, 135
reflexivity, self, 13, 19f., 25f., 26–30, 32f., 68, 138
Robertson, D. B., xv, 114–118, 165
Rubio, Joe, xiv, 145
Rundell, Jay, xiii

Schroeder, P., 96f., 96f.n28, 99n33, 165

Scott, David, xvi, 113n8, 151n20, 163, 166
self, free autonomous, 139f., 160
self, the, 1–33; arrogance of, 3f., 20f. n44, 21, 23, 28, 29, 32, 38f., 43, 75, 81f., 83, 91, 120f.; constituting self, 15, 32f., 68, 127, 131; finitude of, 2f., 18–20, 26–30, 32, 39, 41, 67, 83, 91, 120f., 135; immutable, primordial structure of, 4; self transcendence, self consciousness of, 3, 7, 16, 19, 24, 26, 39, 77; sloth, passivity, self loss, 3f., 23, 28f., 39, 47, 83, 121; vitality and form of, 5–7, 46
Sennett, Richard, and Jonathan Cobb, 27f., 166
Sheehan, Michael, xv, 94–104, 134, 158, 166
Sin, 1n1, 3–5, 20, 32, 38, 43, 46, 54, 71, 72n17, 83; complex weave of, 20–24, 32, 83, 137
Smith, Adam, 55, 55n61, 56n65, 58, 58n73, 59, 166
state, the, 1, 12, 14, 15, 43, 45, 55, 63, 78, 80f., 86, 89–91, 91–94, 99f., 103, 104f., 107, 129, 132, 141n10, 147n16, 148f., 148n17, 152, ; church and state, 152f., 153n21; market state, 107–9
Stone, Ronald H., xvi, 34, 34n6, 52, 69, 70, 71, 85, 91n15, 92, 92n18, 165
Stout, Jeffrey, 141, 141n9, 144n13, 147f.n16, 166
subject, subject-agent, 2, 7–15, 19, 20, 24f., 30, 32f., 54f., 68, 76f., 81–83, 109, 113, 114, 127–32, 132n18, 135, 136, 137–40, 146, 149, 152f., 160
subjectivation, 10, 13, 77

169

Index

subjectivity, 9, 9n22, 12, 13, 20, 26, 32, 66, 67, 127, 127n11, 130, 131, 131n18, registers, layers of, 20, 30–33, 67f., 131, 131n18, 137
survival impulse, 38, 73–75

technologies, 78n29, 80f., 82–84, 94, 102, 106f., 134

Valley Interfaith Project, v, xiv, 145

Weber, Max, 17, 156, 156n22, 166
will to self-realization, 73–75
will to survive, 73–75, 93
Wilson, Jon E., 119–35, 166
Wilson, Woodrow, 98
Wittgenstein, Ludwig, x, 137, 164
Wolin, Sheldon, 139, 139n6, 166
Wolf, William John, 34, 34n4, 166

Zimmerman, Yvonne, xiii, 129n13, 133n20, 149n18

www.ingramcontent.com/pod-product-compliance
Lightning Source LLC
Chambersburg PA
CBHW030111170426
43198CB00009B/577